MOVING FORWARD
DAY BY DAY

MOVING FORWARD

DAY BY DAY

STEPHEN NELSON RUMMAGE

© 2015 by Stephen Nelson Rummage

Published by Moving Forward with Stephen Rummage.

All rights reserved. No part of this book may be reproduced, stored in a retrieval system, or transmitted in any form or by any means—electronic, mechanical, photocopy, recording, or otherwise—without written permission of the author, except for brief quotations in printed reviews.

Unless otherwise indicated, Scripture quotations are from The Holy Bible, English Standard Version Copyright © 2001 by Crossway Bibles, a publishing ministry of Good News Publishers All rights reserved.

ISBN 978-0-9962649-0-7

Printed in the United States of America.

10 9 8 7 6 5 4 3 2

ACKNOWLEDGEMENTS

So many people have played crucial roles in producing this book, and I want to be careful to honor them for their hard work and invaluable contributions.

Kim Jackson, administrative assistant at Moving Forward, joyfully and skillfully accomplishes countless assignments every day for our ministry, including transcribing and editing all my messages for publication. Without her, this book of devotions would not exist. Tracy Sherman also contributed significantly to this project by assisting Kim with coordinating and adapting my sermon materials for use as daily devotions.

Barbie Frost, my executive assistant, keeps my schedule organized and vigilantly guards my time so that I can pray, prepare messages, and preach.

Perry Kosieniak designed the layout and formatted the book's contents. Rachel Hill designed the artwork for the cover jacket. They both did a wonderful job in making this devotional book attractive and easy to use.

Numerous preachers, speakers, and authors I have read and listened to over the years have blessed me with their explanations, illustrations, and applications of the Scripture. Their influence and ideas inevitably shape every sermon I preach. To each of these men of God, I am greatly indebted.

I am extremely grateful for the privilege of preaching God's Word both from the pulpit of Bell Shoals Baptist Church each week and through the Moving Forward broadcast ministry daily. God's people who listen to my messages motivate me to study God's Word and communicate His truth faithfully, day by day.

My precious wife, Michele, and our son, Joshua, are a continual source of joy. The love and encouragement of a godly family, who share a heart for the Lord, His Word, and His people, make ministry a blessing.

To each person I have mentioned, I owe profound thanks and gratitude. To God alone be the glory and praise!

Stephen Nelson Rummage

The Pastor's Study
Bell Shoals Baptist Church
Brandon, Florida
2015

INTRODUCTION

If you've ever gone into a cave or a cavern, you have seen the stalactites, stalagmites, and columns that form as water drips down, leaving behind a deposit of minerals with each drop. Over a long period of time, those drips of water create beautiful and impressive formations of rock. It doesn't happen overnight. It's a cumulative effect.

Things that make the biggest difference in life often depend on cumulative effects. A plant needs to be watered each day in order to grow, rather than being doused with a gallon of water at the beginning of every week. A student who studies and prepares throughout the semester will be more prepared than the one who crams the night before finals. Strong muscles depend on a long-term weight lifting regimen, not one intensive workout session.

Similarly, our life in Christ grows progressively as we follow Jesus day by day. He works in our lives daily to deepen our understanding of His Word, to strengthen our faith in Him, and to increase our holiness and Christ-likeness. Spiritual growth doesn't happen overnight. But it does happen, as we make time to read His Word and pray each day.

There's a simple but profound word the Bible uses to talk about spiritual growth: *progress*. Paul uses the term twice in the New Testament. In 1 Timothy 5:14, he tells Timothy to immerse himself in the study and proclamation of the Scriptures *"so that all may see your progress."* In Philippians 1:25, he expresses his desire to spend time with the believers in Philippi, for the sake of their *"progress and joy in the faith."* The word Paul used often referred to making steady headway on a long journey.

Moving Forward Day by Day is a yearlong devotional book designed to help you make progress spiritually by reading and meditating on God's Word. Each daily reading provides a verse of Scripture to meditate on, an explanation and illustration of the central truth of that verse, a practical application of the biblical truth, and a prayer guide.

Let me encourage you to take time each day to read and think about each verse, to ask how the Scripture applies to your own life and situation, and to pray for God's grace and strength to trust and obey His truth. My prayer is that God will use this book to bless and strengthen your spiritual life.

v

vi

Week 1 — Monday

PERMISSION TO BUILD

Therefore, if anyone is in Christ, he is a new creation. The old has passed away; behold, the new has come.

2 Corinthians 5:17

A businessman was trying to sell a long vacant warehouse. Vandals had damaged the doors, smashed the windows, and piled trash all around the interior.

As the seller showed the prospective buyer around the building, he took great pains to say that the broken windows would be replaced, the structural damage would be repaired, and the garbage taken away.

"Forget the repairs," the buyer said. "I don't want the building; I want the site so I can build something brand new."

Our efforts to improve our own lives are as trivial as sweeping out a warehouse slated for the wrecking ball!

When Jesus saves you, He doesn't intend to make your old life presentable. All He wants is the site and permission to build in you a brand new life. He sweeps away the old and undertakes a brand new construction. Your new life is created to look like Jesus: to think what He thinks, to love what He loves, and to act like He acts.

Don't keep living like the old you. Today, take a good look at the new work that Jesus is doing in you and live accordingly. In Christ, you are brand new!

Lord, thank You for making me a brand new creation! Help me to be submissive and thankful for the wonderful changes You are making in me.

Week 1   Tuesday

HOLD ON

My sheep hear My voice, and I know them, and they follow Me. I give them eternal life, and they will never perish, and no one will snatch them out of My hand. My Father, who has given them to Me, is greater than all, and no one is able to snatch them out of the Father's hand.

John 10:27-29

A little girl had spent the entire day walking hand-in-hand with her father. Together they strolled across meadows, through a dark forest, down a country road, and over the sidewalks of town.

Eventually, they came to a rapidly moving stream. There was no bridge. They would have to walk through the foaming water. The little girl became frightened and anxious.

Her father assured her, "You've held my hand all day. Everywhere we've gone, I've had your hand in mine. When we go through that water, just keep holding my hand."

The little girl held her father's hand tightly, and he brought her safely through.

Are you frightened and anxious when struggles come your way? The same strong and mighty hand of God that guides you on dry land will hold you when you face deep waters. God's hand is strong, comforting, protective, and all powerful. He will never let you go, even in the storms and treacherous waters of life. Nothing can pull you out of His hand.

God is faithful. He will hold your hand in deep waters and walk with you to the other side. He will not let you go.

Father, I trust You to hold on to me through the struggles of life. Thank You that You will never let me go.

Week 1 — Wednesday

DON'T WORRY

Therefore do not be anxious about tomorrow, for tomorrow will be anxious for itself. Sufficient for the day is its own trouble.

Matthew 6:34

A grandfather clock had ticked for years, 2 ticks per second, every minute of every day. But one day the clock began to worry about its responsibilities. It had to tick 7,200 ticks an hour, 172,000 ticks per day, 1,209,600 ticks per week, 62 million ticks a year. It was too much to think about! The clock succumbed to worry and had a nervous breakdown.

The clock saw a psychiatrist for help. The psychiatrist said, "Tell me. How many ticks must you tick at a time?" "I just tick one tick at a time," the clock replied. "Go home and think about ticking one tick," the psychiatrist counseled, "and until you have ticked that tick, don't even think about the next."

What do you worry about? Your family? Your work? Your health? Your finances? Rather than worry, remember that God is loving and sovereign over every circumstance of your life. He knows every situation ahead of time and cares deeply for you. He has control over everything that worries you.

Worry will never change your circumstances, but it will rob you of the joy God wants you to experience. Choose God's joy today and trust tomorrow to Him.

Father, I confess that I worry about so many things. Help me to trust You and trade my worry for Your joy.

Week 1   Thursday

ACCORDING TO HIS RICHES

And my God will supply every need of yours according to His riches in glory in Christ Jesus.

Philippians 4:19

Imagine that Gerald the Squirrel has somehow failed to gather enough acorns. He needs one hundred twenty more acorns to make it through the winter.

Now, Gerald's neighbor in the next tree, Super Squirrel, has somehow stored up five million acorns.

So, Gerald goes to Super Squirrel and asks, "Can you help supply my need of acorns for the winter?"

If Super Squirrel were to supply Gerald's need *from* his riches, he'd give Gerald one hundred twenty acorns. But, if Super Squirrel supplies Gerald's need *according to* his riches, he'll give Gerald an abundant supply of acorns to generously meet his need for the entire winter.

The Bible says that God will supply all of our needs, not *from* His riches, but *according to* His riches in glory in Christ Jesus.

Someone once wrote: "Lord, I crawled across the barrenness to You with my empty cup, uncertain in asking any small drop of refreshment. If only I had known You better, I'd have come running with a bucket!" [1]

Our God is not stingy! Trust His promise that He is able to do so much more than we can even ask or think to meet our needs!

Father, thank You for supplying abundantly for every need I have.

Week 1   Friday

THE GOAL

...Fixing our eyes on Jesus, the author and perfecter of faith, who for the joy set before Him endured the cross, despising the shame, and has sat down at the right hand of the throne of God.

Hebrews 12:2

In 1970, the ill-fated Apollo 13 spacecraft was headed perilously back to earth after a failed lunar mission. To right their course toward home, the astronauts were required to make a critical course correction. If they failed, they might never return to Earth.

Because the on-board computer guidance system had been shut down to conserve energy, the astronauts had to make the course correction manually. This was very difficult and dangerous. Commander Jim Lovell determined if he could keep one fixed point in space in view through the tiny window, he could steer the craft manually. That focal point turned out to be their destination – Earth.

For thirty-nine long seconds, Lovell fought to keep the earth in view. By not losing sight of that reference point, the three astronauts avoided disaster.

Scripture reminds us that to finish our life mission successfully, we need to keep our eyes stayed upon the goal – Jesus Christ. Keeping our eyes fixed on Him will prevent us from drifting off course.

Don't focus on your trials. Instead, focus on Jesus. Keeping your eyes on Him will keep you from veering off course.

Father, sometimes it's hard not to focus on the hard things in life. Today, help me keep my eyes on You so I can stay on the course You have for me.

Week 2   Monday

NEW LIFE

We were buried therefore with Him by baptism into death, in order that, just as Christ was raised from the dead by the glory of the Father, we too might walk in newness of life.

Romans 6:4

A country preacher who preached on baptism all the time was called in by the deacons. "You've got to preach on something else."

He said, "Well, I'd be glad to try. Why don't you pick a text for me?"

The next Sunday, he stood to read the text they had chosen for him: "Even now the axe is laid to the root of the trees. Every tree therefore that does not bear good fruit is cut down and thrown into the fire." (Matthew 3:10) He said, "Why is the ax laid to the root of the trees? So they can build a dam on the creek. And why dam up the creek? To make the water deeper. And why make the water deeper? So folks can get baptized!"

This silly story makes a great point – baptism is a critical step of obedience in the life of every follower of Jesus Christ. Baptism by immersion depicts the death, burial, and resurrection of Jesus Christ. Being baptized identifies us with our Savior.

Scriptural baptism comes after we are saved, not before. Baptism doesn't save you. But if you are saved, you should follow Christ by being baptized. The Bible commands it!

Father, thank You for the opportunity to identify with the Lord Jesus Christ in baptism.

6

Week 2 — Tuesday

EMOTIONS

Indeed, in their case the prophecy of Isaiah is fulfilled that says: "'You will indeed hear but never understand, and you will indeed see but never perceive.' For this people's heart has grown dull, and with their ears they can barely hear, and their eyes they have closed, lest they should see with their eyes and hear with their ears and understand with their heart and turn, and I would heal them.' But blessed are your eyes, for they see, and your ears, for they hear.

Matthew 13:14-16

I watched a guy the other day who was all over the charts emotionally. He was happy one minute, crying the next. He moved quickly from chuckling and singing to stomping his feet in anger. I thought, "This guy is really unbalanced. His personality is unstable. He jumps from one emotion to the other. He needs help." Of course, he was only two years old.

It is normal for spiritually immature people to ride the waves of their emotions. But the Bible says we are to become mature in Christ. How do we do that? There are several ways. We can become aware of God's activity around us by asking Him to open our eyes and give us hearts that are sensitive to the Holy Spirit. We can spend time listening to His voice through prayer and reading His Word. We can keep our affections turned toward Christ.

If we do those things we will live less and less controlled by our emotions and more under the loving control of the Holy Spirit. As you mature in Christ, you will experience a joy that is deeper and greater than your feelings or your circumstances.

Father, I ask that You would help me to grow in You day by day so that I am controlled by You and not my emotions.

Week 2   Wednesday

CONTENTMENT

Not that I speak from want, for I have learned to be content in whatever circumstances I am. I know how to get along with humble means, and I also know how to live in prosperity; in any and every circumstance I have learned the secret of being filled and going hungry, both of having abundance and suffering need. I can do all things through Him who strengthens me.

Philippians 4:11-13

A wealthy man saw a fisherman sitting lazily beside his boat. The sight disturbed the rich man.

"Why aren't you out there fishing? If you catch more fish than you need today, you could earn more money and buy a better boat so you could go deeper and catch more fish. You could purchase nylon nets, catch even more fish, and make more money. Soon you'd have a fleet of boats and be rich like me. Then you could sit down and enjoy life."

The fisherman replied, "What do you think I'm doing now?"

We live in a "never-enough" world that hammers us with the desire to always have better, bigger, and newer. But God desires that we have true contentment, so that whether we have much or little, we can be happy in Him today. What's the secret to this kind of contentment?

The apostle Paul experienced great need many times. But he completely trusted the love of Christ. He knew that whether he lived with abundance of provision or suffered in need, Christ would enable him to have joy and strength in every situation. That's the secret to true contentment.

Father, help me to be content in You in whatever circumstance I experience, whether I have much or little.

Week 2 — Thursday

REST

The apostles returned to Jesus and told Him all that they had done and taught. And He said to them, "Come away by yourselves to a desolate place and rest a while." For many were coming and going, and they had no leisure even to eat.

Mark 6:30-31

I heard about a preacher who would proudly say, "The devil never takes a vacation, so why should I?" He needed a reminder that the devil was not his example to follow.

After a great time of powerful ministry, the disciples reported back to Jesus. God was using them, and Jesus was glad and praised God. And then He said to them, "Come away by yourselves... and rest for a while."

Did you know it's all right for Christians to rest? It's all right for Christians to take a vacation. Jesus gives us permission, even in our service to Him, to occasionally step back for a few moments, or maybe a few days, for some relaxation and rest.

Sometimes we need to rest for health reasons. Sometimes rest helps us avoid ministry burn-out. Rest is often needed to help us guard against a weakness in our lives. Sometimes, we need "down time" just to reconnect with our family and build relationships. We also need restful times to reflect on God's work in our lives.

Don't ignore your need for rest. It might be just what the Great Physician has ordered!

Father, help me to really rest when I need it so I can continue to serve You with joy.

Week 2   Friday

TOGETHER

For just as the body is one and has many members, and all the members of the body, though many, are one body, so it is with Christ. For in one Spirit we were all baptized into one body – Jews or Greeks, slaves or free – and all were made to drink of one Spirit.

1 Corinthians 12:12-13

Famous comedian Jimmy Durante had been invited to entertain a group of World War II veterans. His schedule was completely full but he agreed to a very brief performance.

Mr. Durante wowed the crowd, and to the director's surprise, he remained on stage for a full thirty minutes. Afterward, someone asked the comic, "I thought you only had a few minutes. What happened?"

"Look at the front row," Durante replied. "You'll see why I stayed."

There, seated side by side, were two men. One had lost his right arm in the war, and the other, his left. Together, they were able to clap loudly and cheerfully. Each one happily made up for what the other lacked.

Every person in the body of Christ, the church, is created by God to supply something another member lacks. As we serve together, we grow as a loving body that reflects the complete character of Jesus Christ.

God gives every Christian a gift to use to serve the church. Some are teachers. Some are encouragers. Some are administrators. Some set up tables and chairs. Some feed the hungry. Some take care of children. What gift has God given you to serve His church?

Father, please help me to faithfully use the gift You've given me to serve other believers and strengthen Your church body.

10

Week 3   Monday

DROWNING

Everyone who calls on the name of the Lord will be saved.
Romans 10:13

A basic rule of life saving is that you should not attempt to rescue a drowning person while he is still trying to rescue himself. As long as he's frantically trying to save himself, any effort you make to grab hold of him will give him opportunity to pull you under the water with him.

Lifeguards are taught to stay just within reach of a distressed person until he quits struggling. Then, when he is surrendered and pliable, the rescuer can reach out and save him.

The same thing is true spiritually. Jesus saves people, but only after they have recognized they are powerless to save themselves and they cry out to Jesus, "Lord, save me, a sinner!"

Someone has said that if it costs a dollar to get into Heaven, and God gave you the first 99 cents, you would never be able to make up that last penny. There is nothing we can do to save ourselves. It is futile to try!

The Bible says that Jesus Christ saves every person who calls on His name. We are all spiritually helpless. When you quit trying to save yourself and cry out to Jesus, He will rescue you.

Father, thank You that Jesus saves helpless people like me!

Week 3   *Tuesday*

ARE YOU A RIP VAN WINKLE?

But you are not in darkness, brothers, for that day to surprise you like a thief. For you are all children of light, children of the day. We are not of the night or of the darkness. So then let us not sleep, as others do, but let us keep awake and be sober.

1 Thessalonians 5:4-5

The fictional Rip Van Winkle was lazy and unproductive. To escape his responsibilities at home, he went for a long walk in the woods where he met a group of mysterious men playing games. He took a drink from them and fell asleep for twenty years, missing the colonies becoming a nation, the growth of his children, and the death of his wife. He simply slept his life away.

Many Christians are like Rip Van Winkle. Instead of staying spiritually alert, listening for God's instructions, doing the work of the kingdom, and striving to please their Master, they choose a kind of spiritual sleep. Their spiritual senses are dulled by earthly pursuits and spiritual negligence.

The Bible commands us to be on the alert, to keep watch, to remain sober. If you are spiritually asleep, you need to wake up! Sleepers are in the dark. We are called as children of the light and of the day! Don't miss what God is doing around you, and what He wants to do in and through you.

Jesus is coming soon. Don't be asleep when He gets here. Keep watch. Do the work of the kingdom. Stay on the alert. Wake up!

Lord, I confess that so many times I am asleep on the job. Help me be awake and alert so when You appear, I will be ready and unashamed.

Week 3 — Wednesday

LISTEN

Give ear, O my people, to my teaching; incline your ears to the words of my mouth!

Psalm 78:1

"Listen." It's a simple instruction that parents give to kids, and a life-changing word that God extends to His children.

Psalm 78:1 uses two expressions to call God's people to listen: "give ear" and "incline your ears." Both phrases called for Israel to pay careful attention to what the Lord was about to say. As the Lord spoke to Israel in this historical psalm, He graciously warned them about the cost of rebellion against Him.

When we listen to God, He shows us things we would not otherwise see and alerts us to hazards we would never detect on our own. The two ways we listen to God are through reading His Word and through prayer.

There are so many voices competing for our attention that it's easy not to listen to God. When we stop paying attention to His voice, when we ignore His commands, we will find ourselves in danger.

Today, listen carefully to God as you read His Word and pray. He wants to speak to you of His love, His encouragement, His wisdom, His correction, and His truth.

God is always speaking. Are you listening?

Father, help me to really listen to You today. Help me to hear You speak, and to obey all that You show me.

Week 3   Thursday

THE PRICE HE PAID

For what does it profit a man to gain the whole world and forfeit his soul? For what can a man give in return for his soul?
                                                              Mark 8:36-37

In 2000, a twenty-nine-year-old man auctioned his soul to the highest bidder. After a ten-day bidding war a New York real estate developer won the auction, paying $1325 for the young man's soul.

The seller said he had auctioned his soul to prove a point. "In America," he said, "you can even sell your soul and be rewarded for it. That's what makes this country great."

What is the price for your soul? Jesus says your soul is the most valuable thing you have, because it lasts forever.

Jesus Christ did not come to the bargaining table and negotiate the lowest price for your soul. He willingly paid the only acceptable price: His own life. He took every painful step all the way to Calvary, where Roman soldiers fastened Him to a cross through His hands and His feet. He hung there for six hours, where He suffered and bled and died, all to save your soul from Hell.

God gave overwhelming evidence of His tremendous love for you when His Son, Jesus Christ, paid the price for your soul on the cross of Calvary. No other proof of God's love for you is necessary.

Father, thank You for valuing my soul so much that You paid the highest price to save it and give me eternal life.

14

Week 3   Friday

THE SAME AS US

For we do not have a high priest who cannot sympathize with our weaknesses, but One who has been tempted in all things as we are, yet without sin.

Hebrews 4:15

Father Damien, a Belgian missionary, planted churches on the island of Molokai over one hundred fifty years ago. In a very remote area, he planted a church in a leper colony. With his own hands, Father Damien built a church for the lepers, built houses for them, and helped them create a society for themselves. For fifteen years he lived among them, serving them any way he could.

One day he spilled boiling water on his foot while cooking, but felt no pain. He realized then that he, too, had leprosy. From that moment, Father Damien addressed his friends, not as "my fellow believers," but as "my fellow lepers." He had in every way become one of them, even participating in their suffering.

Jesus will comfort us when we suffer because He suffered. The Son of God became like us in every way, but without sin. He experienced rejection, pain, and sorrow. He experienced separation from God and death when He paid for our sin on the cross.

The best comforter is one who knows what we're going through because he's suffered in same way. Jesus knows exactly what you're going through, and He is completely able to help you through it.

Lord Jesus, I thank You that You know exactly how to comfort me because You suffered, too.

15

Week 4   Monday

SURRENDER

For whoever would save his life will lose it, but whoever loses his life for My sake and the gospel's will save it.

Mark 8:35

In 2005, a young woman's apartment building caught on fire. She could barely breathe as the smoke grew thicker. Her concern grew for her baby boy, who was struggling to breathe.

The young mother held her baby outside a window so he could breathe. She knew her tiny son would not survive a walk down the stairs to the first floor. From the window she saw a man on the sidewalk below, holding out his arms.

Knowing the risk, she let go of her baby boy. The baby fell thirty feet, squarely into the arms of the man, a catcher for the local baseball team. Firemen rescued the mother from the building, and safely reunited her with her infant son.

Her baby's life was saved because she let him go.

If you hold on to your life, you'll lose it. If you try to keep your soul for yourself, you'll lose your soul. But if you come to Jesus on terms of complete surrender, then your life will be saved. It's a paradox, but the truth is we can only truly live when we die.

If you want to save your life, give it over to Jesus. He'll save your life.

Lord Jesus, thank You for Your promise to save my life when I give it completely to You.

Week 4   Tuesday

IRON MOUNTAIN

No temptation has overtaken you that is not common to man. God is faithful, and He will not let you be tempted beyond your ability, but with the temptation He will also provide the way of escape, that you may be able to endure it.

1 Corinthians 10:13

According to legend, there was an island dominated by an iron mountain that emitted such powerful magnetic force that it attracted every piece of metal brought within the range of its influence.

Ships at sea, passing near the rocky shore, felt the mountain pull on their anchors and chains. The closer a ship drew to the land, the stronger the mountain's attraction became, until finally the very nails would fly from the vessel's beams and planks and fasten themselves to the side of the mountain. The doomed ship, of course, would fall to pieces in the sea with great loss of life.

Temptation is like a strong magnet. If you do not keep a safe distance, it will draw you in until it destroys you. Do you find yourself edging dangerously close to sin? Whatever temptation you are facing, flee from it! Get as far away from it as possible. God always provides a way to escape. Leave temptation alone. It can destroy you and all that you hold dear.

Ask for God to give you confidence in Him so that you will cry out to Him in your trials rather using a trial as an opportunity to sin.

Lord Jesus, help me to not give in to temptation today. Help me find the way of escape You have promised.

Week 4   Wednesday

AVAILABLE STRENGTH

But He said to me, "My grace is sufficient for you, for My power is made perfect in weakness." Therefore I will boast all the more gladly of my weaknesses, so that the power of Christ may rest upon me.

2 Corinthians 12:9

A father asked his teenage son to move a heavy rock from one place in their yard to another. The boy strained and grunted, but he couldn't move the rock. His dad stopped and watched for a moment. He said, "Son, you're not using all your available strength."

The boy pushed harder, but still rock didn't budge. Again the father said, "Son, you're still not using all your available strength." The son pushed with all his might, but the rock remained firm.

The exasperated boy said to his dad, "I'm pushing as hard as I can. I don't have any more strength to use."

The father said, "You haven't used all your available strength, because you haven't asked me to help."

God's grace is sufficient for you. It's always enough. Christ's power is perfect when you are weak. All of the power of Christ is available to you to accomplish any task He has given you and to victoriously face any circumstance He allows in your life.

When you are weak, remember that God makes all of His strength available to you. He will always provide His strength to enable you do whatever He asks of you.

Father, forgive me for trying to do Your will in my own strength. Please give me Your strength today to do what You've asked of me.

Week 4   Thursday

HELL IS REAL

And if your eye causes you to sin, tear it out. It is better for you to enter the kingdom of God with one eye than with two eyes to be thrown into Hell, 'where their worm does not die and the fire is not quenched.'

Mark 9:46-48

My wife, Michele, and I had arrived at a crowded restaurant for dinner. As we waited, an irritated couple charged out. The woman hotly announced, "You don't want to go in there! The service is lousy, the staff is rude, the food is cold, and we refuse to eat it."   They marched to the parking lot, as she reiterated, "You don't want to go in there!"

Now everyone waiting had to decide if they would stay or leave. Each person's decision hinged on whether they trusted the testimony of the woman who said, "Don't go in there!"

Jesus Christ has given us a testimony about Hell. He has said Hell is a real place, a fiery place, and it is forever. You don't want to go there.

But there is good news! Jesus Christ, God's Son, died a violent death on the cross of Calvary to pay the price for our sins. On the third day, He rose from the dead. Every person who repents of their sin and calls on Him to save them will not go to Hell, but will be in Heaven with Him forever.

What is your decision? Have you trusted Jesus?

Lord Jesus, I thank You for paying for my sin so that I don't have to spend eternity in Hell, but can live with You forever in Heaven.

Week 4   Friday

DRAIN HOLE

And do not fear those who kill the body but cannot kill the soul.
Rather fear Him who can destroy both soul and body in Hell.

Matthew 10:28

When I was five years old, my greatest fear when I was learning to ride my bike was of storm drains in the road. When I saw one, I would shout out, "Drain hole!" and swerve out into the middle of the road to stay as far away from them as possible.

My father pulled me aside. "Stephen," he said, "you don't need to be scared of the storm drain. You couldn't get into that hole if you tried. But you should be scared that when you swerve into the middle of the road, you could be hit by a car and killed. That's what you should be scared of."

I was confused about what I should fear.

As Christians, the only thing we should fear is disobeying God. We don't have to fear what people can do to us. God is our refuge, our strength, our protector, and defender. In Christ, even if we die, we have His assurance of life beyond the grave.

So don't be afraid of men. Instead, let the fear of disappointing God motivate you to live your life for Him. He can do awesome things through you when you completely entrust yourself to Him.

Father, I confess that sometimes I am more fearful of men than I
am of You. Help me to be fearless of men as I obey You.

Week 5   Monday

JUST ONE THING

And Jesus, looking at him, loved him, and said to him, "You lack one thing: go, sell all that you have and give to the poor, and you will have treasure in Heaven; and come, follow Me." Disheartened by the saying, he went away sorrowful, for he had great possessions.

Mark 10:20-22

As a very young man just starting his business, my dad moved to Greensboro, North Carolina. He lived in a boarding house owned by two elderly sisters. One of the sisters cooked dinner for him every evening, usually keeping him company at the table while he ate.

One night, she brought him a generous slice of an apple pie she had baked for him that day. Steam rose from that freshly baked pie, carrying the homey smell of baked apples. My dad eagerly took a bite. It tasted awful!

Embarrassed, my dad said, "I'm sorry; I just can't eat it." She said, "Oh, I hoped you wouldn't notice. I used salt instead of sugar."

Only one thing was wrong with that pie; just one. In the same way, it only takes one sin to send a person to Hell; just one. God is holy, and He cannot look upon even one sin.

Is just one thing preventing you from following Jesus? The man who knelt before Jesus turned down the opportunity to follow Christ because of just one thing. Don't let anything keep you from following Jesus. Nothing in your life is worth the great cost of not following Him.

Lord Jesus, show me what in my life is keeping me from following You. Help me to set aside that one thing so I can have eternal life with You.

Week 5   Tuesday

AUTOPILOT

Look carefully then how you walk, not as unwise but as wise, making the best use of the time, because the days are evil. Therefore do not be foolish, but understand what the will of the Lord is.

Ephesians 5:15-17

Urban legend tells the story of a man who was driving his brand new RV for the first time. Thinking it was the same thing as an "autopilot," he pushed the cruise control button and stepped to the kitchen of the RV for a drink. Of course, the motor home veered off of the freeway and crashed.

The story may not be true, but the illustration reminds us of the dangers of putting parts of our lives on autopilot. Trying to steer through your life without deliberate effort only leads to mistakes and disappointments.

Are there areas of your life on autopilot? Are you making the best use of your time? Are you investing the precious commodity of time in the kingdom of God and people or wasting it on "stuff?" Don't foolishly ignore God's will for your life in things that seem insignificant, but can land you way off course!

Today, ask God to make evident to you what in your life needs to be changed. It may be as simple as turning off the TV and spending a few extra minutes with your kids or investing yourself in the life of someone at church. Don't drift. Instead, live your life on purpose.

Father, help me to wisely spend the time You give me on what is important to You.

Week 5   Wednesday

A MATTER OF FOCUS

Be sober-minded; be watchful. Your adversary the devil prowls around like a roaring lion, seeking someone to devour. Resist him, firm in your faith, knowing that the same kinds of suffering are being experienced by your brotherhood throughout the world.

1 Peter 5:8-9

Years ago, my son, Joshua, and his Aunt Melissa went to a restaurant where a magician provided entertainment. He asked Joshua and Melissa to assist him in an audience-participation trick. They did all he asked of them and then made their way back to their seats.

When they were again seated, the magician approached them, held up two wristwatches and asked, "Are these yours?" Somehow, he had managed to remove their watches from their wrists without ever being detected!

For Joshua and Melissa, it was all a matter of misplaced focus. The magician used a technique called "misdirection" to draw their attention away so he could remove their watches undetected.

Your adversary, the devil, is a master of misdirection. He often plots to draw your attention away from the important, not to play a harmless trick on you, but to destroy you.

As a born-again child of God, you are to stand firm in your faith and resist Satan. Don't allow Satan's traps of temptation, discouragement, and lies to defeat you today.

Let Jesus answer the door when the devil comes knocking, and remember: Jesus in you is greater than the devil and his tactics.

Father, help me to stand firm against the devil's schemes when he tempts me to take my eyes off of You.

Week 5   Thursday

PRAYING AND BELIEVING

And Jesus answered them, "Have faith in God. Truly, I say to you, whoever says to this mountain, 'Be taken up and thrown into the sea,' and does not doubt in his heart, but believes that what he says will come to pass, it will be done for him. Therefore I tell you, whatever you ask in prayer, believe that you have received it, and it will be yours.

Mark 11:22-24

A little boy had just learned in Sunday school that Jesus said He would give us everything we asked for in prayer. So, standing in his driveway, he prayed: "Lord, I'm asking You to make me fly like Superman. I believe You can do it."

The little boy jumped as high as he could, and thumped back to the ground. Undeterred, he prayed the same prayer again. After several frustrated attempts at flight, he walked away very confused about prayer, and disappointed that God didn't grant his request.

God's promise to answer prayer does not give us a blank check to ask for whatever pops into our mind and expect that we'll receive it.

Jesus gives these instructions in John 15:7. "If you abide in Me, and My words abide in you, ask whatever you wish, and it will be done for you." Jesus' promise to grant our requests is conditional upon our praying according to His will expressed in His Word.

When we pray in faith and according to His will, God is willing to do the impossible, the extravagant, and the unimaginable! So don't be bashful about asking God for the impossible. He really can move mountains!

Father, teach me to pray according to Your will and then help me to wait patiently for Your promised answer.

Week 5

Friday

SPIRITUAL PRIORITIES

Jesus answered, "The most important is, 'Hear, O Israel: The Lord our God, the Lord is one. And you shall love the Lord your God with all your heart and with all your soul and with all your mind and with all your strength.' The second is this: 'You shall love your neighbor as yourself.' There is no other commandment greater than these."

Mark 12:29-31

A love-struck girl gave her beau a beautiful photograph of herself, inscribed on the back with the note, "Dear Jason, I love you with all my heart and soul, forever and ever. Love, Sandy." At the bottom she added, "P.S. If I ever break up with you, I want this picture back."

Though human love often hinges on circumstances, God's love for us never fades or fails. He desires and commands that we love Him in the same way, a way that says, "Lord, no matter what happens, I love You."

We are also to love our neighbors, even those who are unlovable. Your neighbor is anyone God allows across your path. God has shed His love abroad in our hearts so we can love our neighbor, even when they are difficult to love.

Our love for others is the gauge of our love for Jesus. If we don't love others, it shows that we don't really love Jesus, no matter how many times we say we do.

Are you loving God with all your heart, soul, and strength, and loving others as you love yourself? Jesus says that's His priority for you.

Father, forgive me for letting my love for You fade. Help me love You more than anything, and to love my neighbor even when it's hard.

Week 6 — Monday

WHO IS GOD, REALLY?

And this is eternal life, that they know You the only true God, and Jesus Christ whom You have sent.

John 17:3

Psychologists tell us that our mental image of God is largely based on our relationship with our earthly father.

Some people view God as an angry tormenter who spends most of His time being mad at them. Others see God as a strict disciplinarian, just waiting for them to mess up so He can punish them. For some, God is like an absentee father who is too preoccupied to pay attention to them. Still others imagine God to be like a kindly grandfather, indulging them occasionally, but having little in common with them.

These ideas are far from what Scripture teaches us about God's nature and intentions. The night before He died on the cross, Jesus said this to God in prayer: "And this is eternal life, that they know You, the only true God, and Jesus Christ whom You have sent." (John 17:3)

God is knowable! He has given His perfect Word that reveals Himself to us. Instead of relying on your own understanding to tell you what God is like, read His word and spend time in prayer. As you draw near to Him through His Son, Jesus Christ, God will show Himself to you so you can *really* know Him.

Father, I want to know You! As I spend time in Your Word and prayer, please reveal Yourself to me.

Week 6   Tuesday

WORKING OUT YOUR FAITH

Count it all joy, my brothers, when you meet trials of various kinds, for you know that the testing of your faith produces steadfastness.

James 1:2-3

A friend of mine had been a small guy for most of his life. Then, almost overnight, his entire appearance changed! His muscles had become defined and he looked very strong. I asked what he had done to create such a change.

He explained, "I pick a muscle I want to make stronger. When I work out that muscle, l lift a weight again and again until the muscle fails. Then I know the muscle tissue has been torn." He continued. "I let it heal for a couple of days. As it heals it grows back a little thicker and a little stronger. Soon, I see a change in muscle size and strength. It's a painful process, but it works."

Just as lifting weights builds your physical muscles, trusting God in a trial will strengthen your spiritual muscles. Enduring patiently through times of testing strengthens our faith.

No one wants to sign up for additional trials. But God uses the trials that inevitably come our way as valuable "weights" to strengthen us as we trust in Him. So, count it all joy when trials come your way, because they really do make us stronger!

Father, help me to patiently endure the tests You bring my way so my faith will grow.

Week 6 _Wednesday_

KEEP WATCH

Therefore stay awake—for you do not know when the master of the house will come, in the evening, or at midnight, or when the rooster crows, or in the morning—lest he come suddenly and find you asleep.

Mark 13:35-36

On August 8, 1914, Ernest Shackleton, known to his loyal crew as "The Boss," set sail from England with nineteen hardy volunteers aboard a three-masted wooden ship, the _Endurance_, bound for Antarctica to explore the frozen continent.

The adventure stalled in January when the _Endurance_ became icebound in the frozen ocean. Shards of ice pierced the ship's hull, forcing the crew from the ship onto a huge sheet of floating ice. In April, as the waters warmed and the ice began to break apart, they sought shelter on a still frozen island. It was then, when the ocean was again navigable, that the Boss left in a lifeboat with five men, sailing away to find help.

While the Boss was away, Shackleton's second in command admonished the men every morning, "Get your things ready boys. The Boss may come today!" After one hundred five days, the Boss returned to rescue his watchful crew.

Jesus Christ is coming back for us. His return draws closer with each passing day. We are to be alert, anticipating His arrival. We do not know the day or the hour, but we can be sure that He is coming. It could be today! Are you ready?

Father, help me to stay alert and be about Your business every day so that when You return, I'll be ready.

Week 6   Thursday

THE MISSING PIECE

And let steadfastness have its full effect, that you may be perfect and complete, lacking in nothing.

James 1:4

When I was young, my mother visited yard sales in search of bargains. Sometimes she would buy a second-hand jigsaw puzzle for us to put together as a family.

Yard sale jigsaw puzzles have a real upside: they are very inexpensive. But there is also the risk of finding there are pieces missing. You could work on that puzzle for hours, only to discover that the kitten will always have one absent paw, or the covered bridge across the winding creek leads to nowhere. Just one missing piece and the entire picture is incomplete.

Without trials, we are like a yard sale jigsaw puzzle. There are some pieces necessary to our maturity that can only be put in place through the pressures and challenges of life. God uses trials in our lives to create maturity in us that is perfect, complete, and lacking nothing.

We will never become like Jesus Christ if we never suffer. His life was filled with trials, pain, and sorrow. To be like Him means to also be like Him in His suffering. Though we don't wish for trials, we should not regret them because God will use them to perfect and complete us.

Father, thank You that trials and pain in my life are not wasted, but that You use them to make me like Jesus.

Week 6   Friday

IT IS FINISHED

*When Jesus had received the sour wine, He said, "It is finished,"
and He bowed His head and gave up His spirit.*

John 19:30

One day Michele came into our house from the mailbox. She was so excited she was almost skipping. She said, "I just got notification we have paid off our car. It is finished!"

"It is finished" literally means *the debt has been paid.*

We all owe God a debt for our sin that we can never pay. We can never do enough good deeds to pay our debt. The wages of sin is death. We are in a desperate situation.

Jesus Christ completely paid the debt for your sin and my sin on the cross of Calvary. How do we know the debt is paid? Because Jesus said, "It is finished." There is nothing left to be done to cover our sin. He has paid the price in full for us to be saved from God's wrath. This is wonderful news!

Have you called on Jesus and by faith accepted the price He paid for your sin? The Bible says that all who call on the name of the Lord will be saved, because "It is finished!"

*Father, thank You that the debt for my sin has been completely
paid by Jesus!*

Week 7 — Monday

LET GO

Put on then, as God's chosen ones, holy and beloved, compassionate hearts, kindness, humility, meekness, and patience, bearing with one another and, if one has a complaint against another, forgiving each other; as the Lord has forgiven you, so you also must forgive.

Colossians 3:12-13

When my son, Joshua was about two years old, he was given a helium filled balloon at a restaurant. I tied it to his wrist, and he enjoyed it. But after a while, we needed to get rid of the balloon because it interfered with other things.

"Joshua," I said, "how would you like to watch your balloon go really high in the sky?"

He said, "Yeah, Daddy!" So, with him grasping the string in his fist, I untied the balloon.

"Now, let it go," I said. Joshua laughed as he watched the balloon rise into the sky until it disappeared. Then he looked at me and said, "Bring it back." You can imagine what happened next.

Is there someone you need to forgive? When someone hurts us, we can treat the offense like my son's balloon and release it to disappear, or we can hold on to it like a kite that we keep reeling back in.

To truly forgive means to let go of offenses and not reel them back in. That's the kind of forgiveness God extends to us. We are commanded to extend the same forgiveness to others.

Father, help me to forgive _____ today, just as You have forgiven me.

Week 7 — Tuesday

THE BLAME GAME

Let no one say when he is tempted, "I am being tempted by God," for God cannot be tempted with evil, and He himself tempts no one. But each person is tempted when he is lured and enticed by his own desire."

James 1:13-14

Do you ever make excuses for a sin in your life by blaming it on someone or something else? No matter what tempts you, temptation never comes from God.

We play the blame game when we reason, "God allowed me to experience the circumstance where I was tempted, so God tempted me to sin."

The blame game started in the Garden of Eden. When Adam and Eve disobeyed God, Eve blamed the serpent, and Adam blamed Eve. But he didn't stop there. He told God, "The woman You gave me...she gave me fruit ... and I ate." (Genesis 3:12) Adam's excuse was, "God, my sin is really Your fault. After all, You gave me this woman!"

God never tempts us to sin. Rather, God always comes to our aid by providing a clear path of escape when we are tempted. "God is faithful, ...with the temptation He will also provide the way of escape, that you may be able to endure it." (1 Corinthians 10:13)

 Don't make excuses for your sin. Ask God to open your eyes to the way of escape when you face temptation. Then take it!

Father, when I am tempted to sin, help me to see the way of escape You provide and flee from temptation.

Week 7   Wednesday

THE CYCLE OF TEMPTATION

Brothers, if anyone is caught in any transgression, you who are spiritual should restore him in a spirit of gentleness. Keep watch on yourself, lest you too be tempted.

Galatians 6:1

Many things in our world follow a predictable pattern. The sun rises and sets every day. The seasons come and go. Even our minds and bodies follow daily patterns.

Temptation often follows patterns that we can anticipate. Temptation is always attractive. Temptation is tailored to fit our weaknesses. We need to be careful not to place ourselves where we are most likely to be tempted. And when temptation does show up, we need to look for the escape hatch.

When we foolishly give in to temptation, we become entangled in sin, like an insect in a spider web. In the beginning, one sin by Adam brought both spiritual and physical death to every person. Sin can also kill relationships, peace, hopes, and dreams.

Praise God that Jesus has paid for our sin and that He gives us life! We will endure temptation as long as we live. Learn to recognize the patterns of temptation in your life. Stay connected to God through prayer and read your Bible. Listen when the Holy Spirit warns you about temptation, and run from temptation when it arrives. You never have to give in to temptation!

Father, help me to recognize temptation today and run from it!

Week 7   Thursday

POOR IN SPIRIT

And He opened His mouth and taught them, saying: "Blessed are the poor in spirit, for theirs is the kingdom of Heaven."

Matthew 5:2-3

In the early nineties, Donald Trump was nine billion dollars in debt. One day, as he strolled along the streets of New York with his daughter, he pointed to a homeless man and said. "He's better off than I am. Even if he's got absolutely nothing, he has nine billion more dollars than me."

Donald Trump was more than broke, but appearances said otherwise. He still lived in mansions, wore fine suits, and was chauffeured in a limousine. His outward appearance said, "I'm wealthy." But his balance sheet said, "I'm nine billion dollars in debt."

We often do the same thing spiritually. Outward appearances of spirituality, morality, religion, and happiness may portray that everything is okay, but God knows our spiritual balance sheet. Spiritually, we are all bankrupt.

To be poor in spirit means to recognize that you are spiritually destitute apart from God. Followers of Jesus Christ realize that they are totally impoverished apart from God and in need of His grace.

Jesus said those who understand their spiritual poverty are blessed, because God meets every need for those who come to the end of themselves and call on Him.

Father, thank You for helping me see my spiritual poverty apart from Christ. Thank You for giving me the kingdom of Heaven.

Week 7

GETTING REAL ABOUT TEMPTATION

Then desire when it has conceived gives birth to sin, and sin when it is fully grown brings forth death.

James 1:15

In the frigid wilds of Alaska, Eskimos must protect their families and animals from wolves. To kill a wolf, the Eskimo dips a razor-sharp knife in the blood of a seal and sets it outside to freeze. He repeats the process, freezing layer upon layer of blood on the blade. Soon, the knife's blade is hidden like a Popsicle™ stick beneath the frozen blood.

The Eskimo buries the handle of the knife upright in the snow, leaving the blood-covered blade exposed. Eventually the wolf discovers the treat. Over and over, he licks the frozen blood, until his tongue is numb, never feeling the blade cutting his own mouth. In time, the wolf is eating his own blood, becoming weaker and weaker until he collapses and dies.

That story is a powerful illustration of how the temptation to sin works in our lives. We see something that we want. We go after it, disregarding the danger, and wind up reaping the terrible consequences of our sin.

Do not be deceived. Sin, though pleasant for a time, is deadly. Today, ask the Holy Spirit to help you recognize temptation for what it is and to empower you to run away from it!

Father, help me to flee from temptation before I become entangled in sin.

Week 8   Monday

UNDERSTANDING THE RULES

So whether we are at home or away, we make it our aim to please Him. For we must all appear before the judgment seat of Christ, so that each one may receive what is due for what he has done in the body, whether good or evil.

2 Corinthians 5:9-10

Some towns in India hold bicycle races with strange rules. When the starting gun sounds, the riders, as best they can, stay put. Racers are disqualified for tipping over or putting their feet on the ground. When the gun sounds the second time, the rider farthest from the start is the loser, and the person who has moved the least distance from the start is the winner.

It's very important to understand the rules of this race. They are not what we would expect.

The world's rules say that winners are those who have it all together, who are happy all the time, and experience the best things in life.

But Jesus' rules seem backward. "Don't lay up for yourselves treasures on earth... lay up treasure in Heaven ..." "Blessed are you when men revile you and persecute you on my account ..." "Whoever wishes to save his life will lose it, but whoever loses his life for My sake and the gospel's will find it."

We will all stand before Jesus to give an account of how we've lived according to His rules. Jesus' rules are right and true. The world's rules are backward. Whose rules are you living by today?

Lord Jesus, help me to live my life every day according to what pleases You, and not according to the world's rules.

Week 8 — Tuesday

SPIRITUAL SUCCESS

Therefore, my beloved brothers, be steadfast, immovable, always abounding in the work of the Lord, knowing that in the Lord your labor is not in vain.

1 Corinthians 15:58

Former South Carolina football coach Lou Holtz once compared his players to a Kamikaze pilot who flew fifty missions: involved, but not committed. Holtz said a lot of players get involved, but only time will tell if they are really committed to the cause for the good of the team. Only when players are committed can a team be a success.

On a team, in the office, in our homes, and in our churches, some people are involved but never are committed to get the job done, no matter what it takes.

God was so committed to us that He gave His very best, His Son Jesus Christ, to die on the cross for our sins. He deserves nothing less than our whole being. Only by complete commitment to Jesus can we have real spiritual success.

True commitment to Jesus Christ causes us, by His power, to be steadfast in our love for Him and unwavering in our service to Him. We are to abound – to overflow and to flourish – in our work for the kingdom of God. Are you serving God with all you have, or are you just squeaking by?

Father, take my gifts and talents and help me to serve You with gladness and faithfulness.

Week 8 — Wednesday

HAS GOD FORGOTTEN?

Can a woman forget her nursing child, that she should have no compassion on the son of her womb? Even these may forget, yet I will not forget you.

Isaiah 49:15

One day, Sam stopped for fuel at a country gas station. Then he got back in the car, pulled out onto the highway and drove. Sam had driven quite a long way when he noticed that he had left something behind at the gas station: his wife!

He stopped in the next town and asked police to help him get in touch with her. Then Sam called his wife, and admitted, with great embarrassment, that he just hadn't noticed her absence. I'd say she noticed!

Everyone forgets something at one time or another. We forget things like names, where we left our car keys, telephone numbers, or words. And sometimes we forget very significant things like birthdays and anniversaries.

We even forget God. But God never forgets us. He never forgets His Word. He never forgets His promises. He never forgets His covenant with us in Christ.

Don't let hard circumstances make you think God has forgotten you. When we encounter difficulties, especially those that last a long time, it may feel like God has forgotten. But, no matter what you are going through now, or will go through, God will never forget you!

Father, I thank You that You never forget Your children. Thank You that You will never forget me!

Week 8   Thursday

TIME WELL SPENT

For everything there is a season, and a time for every matter under Heaven.

Ecclesiastes 3:1

Imagine an anonymous donor, who loves you very much, has decided to deposit 86,400 pennies into your account every morning, starting tomorrow. That's $864 a day; almost $315,000 a year.

The only stipulation is that you must spend all 86,400 pennies every day. No balances can be carried from day to day.

Now let's talk about reality. Every morning, God deposits into your day 86,400 seconds. That's twenty-four hours each of us has to spend every day. However, time can never be carried over. There are no accruals. Nor can we get it back if we spend it regretfully.

Someone has said, "Life is like a coin. You can spend it any way you want to, but you can spend it only once."

Time is a precious treasure that God gives you. There is enough time for every task God has given you to accomplish. So be careful how you spend your time. Make the best use of your time to make the best use of your life.

Today, spend every second for the purpose of glorifying God. That will always be time well spent.

Father, I confess that sometimes I waste time. Thank You that You give me all the time I need to do what You give me to do.

Week 8   Friday

A MATTER OF PERSPECTIVE

Ascribe to the LORD the glory due His name; worship the LORD in the splendor of holiness.

Psalm 29:2

The mountains of North Carolina are beautiful in every season. But our family enjoys the mountains most in the summer when the temperatures are warm. We enjoy time simply gazing at the mountains during the day until the sun sets behind them. At night we listen to the songs of crickets and frogs.

During the day, the leaves, the billowy clouds, the babbling brook, song birds and majestic eagles, and all woodland creatures point to the greatness of God. All creation is a reflection of His matchless character. Creation itself worships our amazing Creator.

The hymn, "All Creatures of Our God and King" expresses this worship wonderfully:

> All creatures of our God and King
> Lift up your voice and with us sing,
> Alleluia! Alleluia!
> Thou burning sun with golden beam
> Thou silver moon with softer gleam!
> O praise Him! O praise Him!
> Alleluia! Alleluia! Alleluia!
> Let all things their Creator bless
> And worship Him in humbleness,
> O praise Him! Alleluia!
> Praise, praise the Father, praise the Son
> And praise the Spirit, Three in One!
> O praise Him! O praise Him!
> Alleluia! Alleluia! Alleluia!

Father, I praise You for Your wonderful creation!

Week 9   Monday

PARDON

Who is a God like You, pardoning iniquity and passing over transgression for the remnant of his inheritance? He does not retain His anger forever, because He delights in steadfast love.

Micah 7:18

In 1830, a man named George Wilson was convicted of robbing the U.S. Mail, a crime that carried the penalty of death. President Andrew Jackson issued a pardon for Mr. Wilson. Amazingly, George Wilson refused to accept it.

What was to be done with a man under the sentence of death who refused a presidential pardon? The Supreme Court heard the case. Their decision was this – a pardon refused is no pardon at all. George Wilson was hanged.

We call George Wilson a fool for rejecting a pardon that would have set him free. However, those who reject Jesus Christ do exactly the same thing.

Jesus Christ has met every requirement for you to be saved. His death and resurrection make the way for you to be forgiven for every sin, for your heart to be cleansed, and for you to have peace with God.

Have you received that pardon or do you reject it? Remember, a pardon refused is no pardon.

If you have never come to Jesus Christ to be saved, He invites you to come to Him today. He loves you and wants to save you!

Father, I confess I am a sinner in need of Your forgiveness. I ask You to save me and give me Your gift of eternal life. Thank You for pardoning my sin through the death of Your Son, Jesus Christ.

Week 9   Tuesday

ARE YOU READY?

It is appointed for man to die once, and after that comes judgment.

Hebrews 9:27

A woman in a job interview was asked, "I see your birthday is April 12. What year?" Without blinking an eye, she smiled and replied, "Every year." That was a smart lady! She answered the question well and received the job.

Every day, we're all moving closer to our last day on earth. At the end of our lives, each person must answer only one question – "What have you done with God's Son, Jesus Christ?"

If you have placed your faith in Him to save you from your sin, you will live in Heaven forever with Jesus. You will enjoy eternity with Him in paradise.

If you have not trusted Christ, Jesus will say to you those words none us of wants to hear: "I do not know where you come from. Depart from Me, all you workers of evil!" (Luke 13:27)

No person will enter Heaven without Jesus Christ. You have today to call on Jesus, but you are not promised tomorrow. Call on Jesus Christ to save you right now. Don't put it off! He wants to save you from the penalty of your sin and give you a brand new life. Don't enter eternity without Jesus!

Father, thank You for my salvation. Help me tell someone who needs to be saved about Jesus today.

42

Week 9   Wednesday

EYESIGHT OR MEMORY

Though you have not seen Him, you love Him. Though you do not now see Him, you believe in Him and rejoice with joy that is inexpressible and filled with glory...

1 Peter 1:8

President Ronald Reagan told the story of an eighty-year-old golfer who was hampered by failing eyesight. He could still hit the ball, but he couldn't see where it went. So, his doctor teamed him with a ninety-year-old man who had perfect eyesight and was willing to be the golfer's spotter.

The eighty-year-old man hit the first ball and asked his companion if he saw where it landed. "Yep." said the ninety-year-old.

"Where did it go?" the eighty-year-old demanded.

The ninety-year-old replied, "I don't remember."

So many people won't believe what they can't see. But Jesus Christ calls us to exercise our faith in Him even though we've not seen Him.

The prophets of the Old Testament were told that the Messiah would come but did not live to see it. They believed what they could not see. We have the benefit of the testimony of those who touched and heard and saw and walked with Jesus. We have the assurance of the Holy Spirit and the truth of God's Word.

One day our faith will be made sight. But until that day, we can rejoice because we know Jesus Christ!

Father, thank You that one day I will see You! Thank You that, though I can't see You, You are working in my life.

Week 9   Thursday

HIS HAPPINESS

But the fruit of the Spirit is love, joy, peace, patience, kindness, goodness, faithfulness, gentleness, self-control; against such things there is no law.

Galatians 5:22-23

Bronnie Ware is a hospice nurse who cares for patients in their final weeks of life. Dying patients express clarity of focus and vision that perhaps they have not had before, often expressing regrets about their lives. One of the most often mentioned regrets Bronnie has heard from her patients is, "I wish I'd let myself be happier."[2]

So many people at the end of their lives think, "If I just hadn't worried so much, if I just hadn't let everything get to me. I wish I had lived happier."

It's good to be happy, but God desires much more than that for us. He wants us to have great joy. Happiness depends on circumstances, which can often go from wonderful to devastating in a moment. But real joy comes from having new life and hope in Jesus Christ. Abiding joy comes from delighting ourselves in Him and living to please Him. True joy does not change with your circumstances.

God's Son, Jesus Christ, came to earth, died upon the cross, and rose from the grave so you can experience God's forgiveness, grace, mercy, peace, and have real joy in your life.

Lord Jesus, thank You that true joy comes from You, not from my circumstances.

Week 9   Friday

WISE COUNSEL

*Let the wise hear and increase in learning, and the one who
understands obtain guidance.*

Proverbs 1:5

The CEO of any company will probably tell you how
important it is to have a dependable and trustworthy
board of directors. No one is "omni-competent." Great leaders
understand they don't know everything. They surround
themselves with capable people who can guide them in their
decisions.

The same is true in other aspects of our lives. Even the very
best of us has blind spots and areas of weakness. We need
people in our lives who can help us make wise and good
decisions and who can warn us when we are making foolish
choices.

The best kind of person to listen to is someone who offers
godly counsel based on God's Word, the Bible. These are the
people in your life you can trust to correct you when you are
going in the wrong direction. They are the ones with whom
you can share the details of your spiritual and moral life, who
will give frank and honest advice, and who will pray with you
about your greatest struggles and challenges.

Make every effort to surround yourself with counselors who
walk closely with Jesus Christ and who will guide you wisely.

---

*Father, I need godly counselors in my life. Please show me the
right people to ask when I need wisdom and guidance.*

Week 10   Monday

REAL SATISFACTION

For He satisfies the longing soul, and the hungry soul He fills with good things.

Psalm 107:9

Most parents of newborns learn very early what sounds their baby makes when hungry. Most moms and dads quickly become very adept at identifying the hunger cry. When the baby sounds the alarm, out comes the food to meet the need. But sometimes, the baby is given a pacifier to make everything okay...for a little while.

A pacifier is simply fake food, a piece of rubber carefully designed to trick the child. Eventually, the baby realizes the pacifier isn't meeting the real need and isn't shy about letting you know he wants the real thing.

Many people spend their lives trying to meet their deep hungers with things that don't satisfy. Things like money, achievement, romance, sex, education, music, and preaching can make us feel better immediately, and gratify us temporarily, but they never bring lasting satisfaction.

We all have a deep spiritual hunger that can only be quieted by a relationship with God through Jesus Christ. God longs to meet the deepest needs of your soul. Don't live being pacified by things that don't truly satisfy. Let Jesus truly satisfy the longings of your heart.

Lord Jesus, You are the only one who can really satisfy me. Forgive me for trying to satisfy my needs with other things.

Week 10 — Tuesday

WHEN YOU PASS THROUGH THE WATERS

But now thus says the Lord, He who created you, O Jacob, He who formed you, O Israel: "Fear not, for I have redeemed you; I have called you by name, you are Mine. When you pass through the waters, I will be with you; and through the rivers, they shall not overwhelm you; when you walk through fire you shall not be burned, and the flame shall not consume you.

Isaiah 43:1-2

In 2010 a terrible rain storm devastated Nashville, Tennessee, and the surrounding area. Homes were flooded, some all the way to the rooftop.

One family experienced a double crisis when the wife went into labor in her home, which was by now surrounded on all sides by water. A doctor was located a few miles away, but the torrent of floodwater seemed impassable. He would have to walk through the rapidly moving current to reach the laboring mom.

Amazingly, he made it to the woman's home, and delivered the baby by flashlight. He rescued the mom and the baby in the middle of the storm.

Life is full of storms. Some are predictable. Some seem to arise from nowhere and quickly lead to desperation. Storms in your health, the welfare of your children, your job, your finances, and your relationships can be devastating and cause you to fear.

Remember, God can safely navigate every storm. When the waters rise, He is with you and He will never leave you nor forsake you. He can lead you safely through your storm. So don't be afraid. Jesus is the Lord of the storm. He will keep you safe.

Father, thank You that You are greater than any storm in my life.

Week 10   Wednesday

TRULY A MIRACLE

Seek the Lord and His strength; seek His presence continually!
Remember the wondrous works that He has done, His miracles
and the judgments He uttered, O offspring of Israel His servant,
children of Jacob, His chosen ones!

1 Chronicles 16: 11-13

On Wednesday, May 12, 2010, a jetliner en route from Johannesburg to Tripoli crashed as it attempted to land in Libya. A security official said the plane had "exploded on landing and totally disintegrated."

All aboard – about one hundred men, women and children – were killed except for one child, a young boy from the Netherlands. Many people said the child's survival was "truly a miracle."

If you are saved, God has done a miracle in your life. When you were spiritually dead, He raised you to new life when you trusted Jesus Christ. His Holy Spirit dwells in you, leading you and guiding you. Don't forget what a miracle it is that, having once been dead in trespasses and sins, you are now alive in Jesus Christ and have been saved by grace!

Sometimes God does miracles in our circumstances. Does He always do miracles in answer to our requests? No, but God always wants us to ask. He is still able to do abundantly more than we can ask or imagine! Praise the Lord that He is still in the miracle working business.

Father, thank You for the miracle of new life in Jesus Christ!

Week 10   Thursday

CAN YOU BE TRUSTED?

One who is faithful in a very little is also faithful in much, and one who is dishonest in a very little is also dishonest in much. If then you have not been faithful in the unrighteous wealth, who will entrust to you the true riches?

Luke 16:10-11

A new pastor in town one day rode the city bus from his home to the downtown area. He paid his fare and went to his seat, where he discovered the driver had given him too much change. He thought to himself, "*You'd better give that back. It would be wrong to keep it.*" Then he thought, "*Forget it, it's only a quarter. The bus company overcharges anyway.*"

When his stop came, he paused momentarily at the door, then handed the quarter to the driver and said, "Here, you gave me too much change."

The driver smiled and said, "Aren't you the new pastor in town?" He said, "Yes, sir, I am."

The driver replied, "I need to get back to church. When you came on today, I decided to give you twenty-five cents too much to see what you would do with it." He then said, "I'll see you in church on Sunday."

How we handle our money and material possessions reveals the motives of our hearts and proves our trustworthiness with God's provisions. Not only is God watching, but others are watching us as well. Can you be trusted?

Father, help me to be faithful and trustworthy with all that You provide me.

Week 10

Friday

LAW OF THE HARVEST

Do not be deceived: God is not mocked, for whatever one sows, that will he also reap.

Galatians 6:7

A young man wanted to aggravate the hard-working farmer who lived down the road. He and some of his friends sneaked into the farmer's field one night and scattered crabgrass seed all over the farm. Soon, the crabgrass sprouted. The young man kept an eye on the farmer, laughing at him every time he saw him working in the fields, hopelessly trying to get rid of the pesky intruder.

A few years later, the now fully grown man, who had long ago forgotten his teenage prank, fell in love with the farmer's daughter and married her. When the father died, the son-in-law inherited the farm, and the crabgrass. For the rest of his life he reaped the crabgrass he had sown all those years ago.

Our actions always produce repercussions in our lives. When we disobey God, there will be consequences. It's the law of the harvest. If you plant a watermelon, you'll never reap green beans. The harvest will always produce what you've sown.

What seeds are you sowing today? Are you sowing good seed? The seeds you plant today will reap either a good or a bad harvest for the rest of your life. Make sure you plant good seed.

Father, help me to sow seeds that will reap a harvest of good things from You in my life.

Week 11 — Monday

A CERTAIN SALVATION

Blessed be the God and Father of our Lord Jesus Christ! According to His great mercy, He has caused us to be born again to a living hope through the resurrection of Jesus Christ from the dead, to an inheritance that is imperishable, undefiled, and unfading, kept in Heaven for you, who by God's power are being guarded through faith for a salvation ready to be revealed in the last time.

1 Peter 1:3-5

A very concerned man came to his pastor and said, "Pastor, I'm just not sure whether I'm saved. I called on Jesus to save me, but I've done some things that I know are wrong, and I'm just not sure. Am I still saved?"

The pastor said, "You know, my dog never makes a mess on the carpet. He obeys when I say 'come.' He can play dead. He can shake my hand. That dog is obedient." Then he said, "In the kitchen is my two-year-old son. He took a red crayon and colored all over our living room wall. He disobeys. He screams and he cries. But if I die today, this dog doesn't get my inheritance. My son does, because he's my son."

God doesn't save good people. There are no good people. God saves sinners who can never be good enough. Our certain salvation comes by faith in the death, burial, and resurrection of Jesus Christ. A genuine salvation cannot be lost because it cannot be earned. It is a gift of God's grace alone. If you have truly been saved, God will not let you go. You can count on His promise.

Father, thank You that my salvation is secure because it's a gift from You, not a reward for good behavior.

Week 11   Tuesday

THERE IS HOPE

For I know the plans I have for you, declares the Lord, plans for welfare and not for evil, to give you a future and a hope.

Jeremiah 29:11

A hospital tutor, assigned to a severely burned boy to keep him from falling further behind in school, was overcome as she cautiously approached his bedside. The boy's face was hardly recognizable. His hands and feet were angry and swollen. Finally, she gathered enough composure to stammer along briefly about nouns and verbs. The hurting little boy was completely unresponsive to her efforts. She left, feeling defeated and unable to help him.

The tutor came every day. Within weeks, the boy had improved significantly and become a model patient. The teacher appeared to be a miracle worker, though all she had done was teach him a little every day about nouns and verbs. When the nurses questioned the boy about his turnaround, he answered, "I figured they wouldn't send somebody to teach a dying boy." The boy had found hope.

The resurrection of Jesus Christ gives us a living hope that cannot fade away! It gives hope when you lose your job, when your marriage is troubled, when you are confined to a hospital bed, and even when you encounter death. We have the greatest hope there is. Today, let us live like it!

Father, thank You for the living hope that I have in Jesus Christ!

Week 11   Wednesday

FADING AWAY

Blessed be the God and Father of our Lord Jesus Christ! According to His great mercy, He has caused us to be born again to a living hope through the resurrection of Jesus Christ from the dead, to an inheritance that is imperishable, undefiled, and unfading, kept in Heaven for you...

1 Peter 1:3-4

Everything on earth is fading away.

The car in your driveway – the one with the new car smell – is one day going to end up in a junk yard, waiting to be crushed and sold for scrap. Its parts will be melted down and used for something else. That's the destiny of the most beautiful and expensive car on the road today.

Our homes, our possessions, our bodies – everything in this world is perishing.

But be encouraged! The life, death, and victorious resurrection of Jesus Christ bring us an enduring inheritance – eternal life with Him in Heaven. If you are trusting Jesus Christ alone for salvation, you have an inheritance that will never fade away. It will not tarnish or become dull. It will never spoil or perish. It has no expiration date. It never loses its value or beauty. And it is reserved in Heaven for you!

This inheritance is a certain one, but is only available to those who've placed their faith in Jesus Christ.

Today, if you are discouraged that the world is fading around you, focus on the inheritance that is yours in Christ. It has your name on it and is waiting for you!

Lord, none of my possessions on earth will last. Thank You for the wonderful inheritance You have waiting for me in Heaven.

Week 11 — Thursday

LIFE, DEATH AND VICTORY

...for a little while, if necessary, you have been grieved by various trials, so that the tested genuineness of your faith—more precious than gold that perishes though it is tested by fire—may be found to result in praise and glory and honor at the revelation of Jesus Christ.

1 Peter 1:6-7

One Wednesday, I spent thirty-four hours flying home from Central Asia. On Wednesday morning I boarded an airplane at 9:00 a.m. I landed at 10:00 a.m. on Wednesday. I took off again at noon on Wednesday, and landed at 5:00 p.m. on Wednesday. Then I boarded a plane for the last leg home and landed at 8:30 p.m. - you guessed it - on Wednesday. It was the longest Wednesday of my life.

My neck hurt. I needed to shave. I was tired, and not happy. But when I finally saw my wife, Michele, at the pickup area with our son, Joshua, in the back seat, it no longer mattered how long my Wednesday had been. As soon as I saw those I loved, I rejoiced!

The Bible says we can have an overcoming joy even when we undergo trials, because we look forward to seeing Jesus when He returns. Followers of Christ have a living hope that makes us able to rejoice in every trial, even the most painful ones.

Remaining faithful to Jesus while we experience trials proves the genuineness of our faith and will bring praise and glory to Jesus. So why not rejoice today? He'll be back soon!

Father, I look forward to seeing Jesus when He returns for me!

Week 11

The Perfection of Jesus

...God anointed Jesus of Nazareth with the Holy Spirit and with power. He went about doing good and healing all who were oppressed by the devil, for God was with Him.
Acts 10:38

The newly engaged young lady showed her diamond ring to her mother. Her mother asked, "Do you love this man?"

"Oh yes," replied her daughter, "he's perfect. And the diamond is perfect, too!" Her mother wisely said, "You may be half right. The diamond may be flawless, but the man never is!"

Diamonds are considered flawless when they reveal no visible imperfections. But even as a flawless diamond shows its faults when magnified sufficiently, everything and everyone on this sinful earth has flaws.

Most of us are like the Grand Canyon – we look best when viewed from a distance. Get too close and our flaws show.

However, the life of Jesus Christ was completely flawless. He was fully God and fully man. He never sinned, not even once. God anointed Him with His Holy Spirit and power, and God was with Him.

The complete perfection of Jesus Christ makes His death on the cross the only acceptable payment for our sin. Today, give thanks that Jesus Christ, who never sinned, gave His perfect life to pay the price for yours!

Lord Jesus, thank You for Your sinless life that was laid down to pay for my sin.

Week 12   Monday

THE FATHER'S SACRIFICE

For God so loved the world, that He gave His only Son, that whoever believes in Him should not perish but have eternal life. For God did not send His Son into the world to condemn the world, but in order that the world might be saved through Him.

John 3:16-17

In 1937, John Griffith brought his eight-year-old son, Greg, to work with him at a drawbridge. They enjoyed the morning together, with John occasionally raising the bridge for the boats to pass. At lunch time, they descended to an observation platform to eat. After a while, John glanced at his watch. The Memphis Express train would soon come barreling down the tracks.

John left Greg and ran to the controls. When he looked to check for boats approaching the bridge, he was horrified to see that Greg had fallen from the platform, and his leg was stuck in the gearbox of the drawbridge.

John had no time to rescue Greg. The train with four hundred people aboard was coming quickly. With unimaginable grief, John pushed the lever to lower the bridge, sacrificing the life of his precious son to save the lives of people who might never know the price that had just been paid so they could live.

God sacrificed His Son, Jesus Christ, on a cross so you could have eternal life. Don't ignore the tremendous sacrifice that was made so you could live. God gives eternal life to every person who places their faith in Jesus Christ!

Father, thank You for Your great love for me and the sacrifice of Your only Son so I could have life.

Week 12   Tuesday

FATHER FORGIVE THEM

And when they came to the place that is called The Skull, there they crucified Him, and the criminals, one on His right and one on His left. And Jesus said, "Father, forgive them, for they know not what they do." And they cast lots to divide His garments.

Luke 23:33-34

A man in Asia had come to faith in Jesus Christ. He was ostracized by family and friends. Perhaps the hardest thing he had to do as a new disciple of Christ was to forgive a man who had hurt his family deeply. His mother had been raped by her own nephew – the man's first cousin.

He knew he needed to forgive his cousin for this unthinkable act of violence. He prayed, "Jesus, help me to forgive my cousin." Wonderfully, God gave this man the grace to forgive.

Forgiveness sounds like a great idea until you're the one who has to do it. Jesus is our example. On the cross, surrounded by the hateful jeers of the mocking crowd, the Son of God compassionately prayed, even as He was dying, "Father, forgive them."

When humanity was at its absolute worst, Jesus pleaded not for justice and punishment, but for mercy and grace for those who hurt Him the most.

Because Jesus forgave, we know that we are to forgive. God's grace and power are always available for us to extend forgiveness to others. Who is Jesus calling you to forgive today?

Father, thank You that You give me the power to forgive those who have hurt me.

Week 12   Wednesday

TODAY ... IN PARADISE

One of the criminals who were hanged railed at Him, saying, "Are you not the Christ? Save Yourself and us!" But the other rebuked him, saying, "Do you not fear God, since you are under the same sentence of condemnation? And we indeed justly, for we are receiving the due reward of our deeds; but this Man has done nothing wrong." And he said, "Jesus, remember me when You come into Your kingdom." And He said to him, "Truly, I say to you, today you will be with Me in Paradise."

Luke 23:39-43

Every time you see a person with a cigarette held to his lips, you can be assured of one thing: he has ignored a clear warning that smoking cigarettes can kill you.

However, if you don't ever smoke, you will still die. Life carries this warning label: "You will die." For some, however, death is looming just moments ahead.

Two criminals were dying on either side of Jesus. One was unrepentant, slandering and blaspheming Jesus until the very end. The other criminal, however, acknowledged his guilt and recognized Jesus' innocence. Most importantly, he asked Jesus to save him: "Lord, remember me when You come into Your kingdom."

What a wonderful promise our Lord made to the repentant thief! Though he still suffered all the pain of death, this thief lived his remaining moments with Jesus' assurance that the instant he died, he would be with Jesus in paradise.

Which side of the cross are you on: the lost side or the saved side? We are all dying. Whether we go to Heaven or Hell depends on one thing alone – what have we done with Jesus?

Lord Jesus, thank You for Your great promise of eternal life for those who call on You.

58

Week 12 — Thursday

FAMILY REDEFINED

When Jesus saw His mother and the disciple whom He loved standing nearby, He said to His mother, "Woman, behold, your son!" Then He said to the disciple, "Behold, your mother!" And from that hour the disciple took her to his own home.

John 19:26-27

Mary must have experienced overwhelming grief as she watched her Son, Jesus suffer a violent death on the cross. She saw the soldiers and crowds mock Jesus. Mary saw the pain and anguish Jesus was enduring. Her heart broke as she helplessly watched her Son die. John accompanied Mary at the cross, and was now responsible to care for her.

Writing some years later, John summarized what he did: "from that hour, the disciple took her to his own home." (John 19:27)

John didn't just give Mary a room in his house or a place at his table, or an open invitation to holiday celebrations. John took Mary to his own family. Jesus' mother became John's mother. And John loved Mary because John loved Jesus.

At the cross, Jesus reminds us that He came to expand what family really is. Believers in Jesus Christ are now joined together as brothers and sisters related by blood – the blood of Jesus! The church is not *like* a family; the church *is* a family called to minister to each other with the love of Christ.

Father, thank You for making me part of Your family in Christ!

Week 12   Friday

RELATIONSHIPS

Now from the sixth hour there was darkness over all the land until the ninth hour. And about the ninth hour Jesus cried out with a loud voice, saying, "Eli, Eli, lema sabachthani?" that is, "My God, My God, why have You forsaken Me?"

Matthew 27:45–46

When my friend, John, retired after thirty years as a teacher and coach, hundreds of current and former students, school officials, and friends turned out for the dedication of a new athletic center being named after him. John's opening words in his speech were, "It's all about relationships. And the relationship that motivates me most is my relationship with Jesus Christ."

The perfect relationship Jesus shared with God the Father makes His cry from the cross all the more painful to hear. As He hung upon the cross, His Father turned away from Him. Jesus cried out in anguish: "My God, My God, why have You forsaken Me?" Jesus' anguished cry revealed the depth of His breaking heart.

Jesus became our sin and endured sin's penalty - total separation from God. He was forsaken by God so that you and I will never be.

Because Jesus was willing to be forsaken by His Father on the cross, we can have a close, personal, and eternal relationship with God. It's all about relationships. God loved you so much that He endured the ultimate pain and abandonment so that you can be His forever!

Father, thank You that because Jesus was forsaken on the cross, You will never forsake me!

Week 13   Monday

I THIRST

After this, Jesus, knowing that all was now finished, said (to fulfill the Scripture), "I thirst." A jar full of sour wine stood there, so they put a sponge full of the sour wine on a hyssop branch and held it to His mouth.

John 19:28–29

We've all been thirsty. Water is required to live. God has placed the signal of thirst within our bodies so we will drink. But what did it mean for Jesus Christ, the Water of Life, to say, "I thirst"?

It meant that the end of His life was very near. Only a few more moments remained until the payment for our sin would be made in full.

It meant that Scripture was fulfilled. David had prophesied of the suffering Christ in Psalm 69: "I am weary with my crying out; my throat is parched. My eyes grow dim with waiting for my God.... They gave me poison for food, and for my thirst they gave me sour wine to drink."

It meant that Jesus fully experienced the pain and suffering of this world. The words, "I thirst," stand as a powerful reminder that when we are in need, in pain, alone, helpless, exposed, and suffering, Jesus has been there and can empathize with us

Is your soul thirsty? Jesus experienced the greatest thirst so He could forever satisfy yours. He gives living water to all who ask Him.

Lord Jesus, I believe You are living water for my soul. Only You can satisfy my thirst.

Week 13   Tuesday

TWO FINAL WORDS

*When Jesus had received the sour wine, He said, "It is finished,"
and He bowed His head and gave up His spirit.*

John 19:30

*Then Jesus, calling out with a loud voice, said, "Father, into Your
hands I commit My spirit!" And having said this He breathed His
last.*

Luke 23:46

African Christians often pray to die "a good death." This
does not mean dying without pain, or even dying at an
old age.

Dying a good death means having the opportunity to have
your family around you before you die to express your love to
them, to charge them to live for Jesus Christ, and to prepare
for a reunion in Heaven.

Jesus Christ died a good death, though it was painful and
humiliating. His death purchased life for everyone who trusts
in Him.

The statement, "It is finished," proclaimed that Christ's work
of redemption was complete. At that moment, everything that
needed to be done for us to be saved had been done. The
mission was accomplished.

"Father, into Your hands I commit My spirit" is a message of
submission. Though the cross was brutal, Jesus' life was not
taken from Him. He gave His life willingly, freely, and by His
own power.

Jesus' death was a good death because it brought life to all
who believe on Him.

---

*Lord Jesus, thank You so much for the good death You died so
that I could live.*

Week 13 — Wednesday

HOLLOW

Now if Christ is proclaimed as raised from the dead, how can some of you say that there is no resurrection of the dead? But if there is no resurrection of the dead, then not even Christ has been raised. And if Christ has not been raised, then our preaching is in vain and your faith is in vain.

1 Corinthians 15:12-14

Many of us have received chocolate bunnies on Easter Sunday. Have you ever excitedly bitten into the ears of your chocolate bunny, expecting a thick, wonderful treat, only to have the bunny's ears crumble into a pile of pieces and crumbs? What a disappointment to find out that your chocolate bunny is just a hollow shell.

The message of Christianity is hollow if Jesus has not been raised from the dead. If Jesus is still in the grave, He is not God. If there is no resurrection, then there is no gospel, no forgiveness, no salvation, and no life after death. Without the resurrection, we have no hope.

But Jesus was gloriously raised from the dead! He is alive today and is seated at the right hand of God. He conquered sin, death, and Hell! Our risen Savior gives eternal life to all who place their faith in Him. The resurrection of Jesus Christ gives us assurance for today and hope for tomorrow. Because Jesus lives, so shall we!

When you tell people about Jesus, make sure and tell them about the resurrection. The gospel is empty without the resurrection.

Father, thank You that Jesus is alive and that we have everlasting hope because He was raised from the dead.

Week 13   Thursday

WHEN GOD SURPRISES YOU

And entering the tomb, they saw a young man sitting on the right side, dressed in a white robe, and they were alarmed. And he said to them, "Do not be alarmed. You seek Jesus of Nazareth, who was crucified. He has risen; He is not here. See the place where they laid him.

Mark 16:5-6

Sometimes, when I come home, I hear Michele vacuuming somewhere in the house. So I close the door very gingerly and sneak to the room where she's working, quietly standing in the doorway until she sees me. Of course, she is usually startled when she finally notices me. It's one of the few surprises I can get by with.

When the women arrived at the tomb of Jesus on the third day, His body wasn't there. Instead, an angel sat beside the place where His body should have been. The women were shocked! It was the greatest surprise they would ever experience.

God has the right to surprise you. God is always doing something new, something unexpected, something that may even be alarming to us. We must trust God and respond in faith to His surprises, saying, "Lord, though this is a surprise to me, I know it's what You want, so I will obey You."

Have you surrendered to God's surprises? Whether they are joyful or difficult in the beginning, they are always for the purpose of teaching us to trust Him and to accomplish His purposes in our lives.

Father, help me to gladly obey You when You surprise me with something new.

Week 13

Hope Comes Home

And he said to them, "Do not be alarmed. You seek Jesus of Nazareth, who was crucified. He has risen; He is not here. See the place where they laid Him.

Mark 16:6

Violet and Samuel walked through the countryside, their wedding only weeks away. An argument arose, and, in an angry moment, Violet threw her engagement ring across the field where it became stubbornly lost in the grass. The couple quickly reconciled, but the ring was never found.

The story of the lost ring became a family legend during Violet and Samuel's fifty-two year marriage. After Samuel passed away, one of their grandsons searched the legendary field with a metal detector. In only two hours, the ring was found. He had it cleaned until it sparkled and returned it to Violet. Violet slid the ring back onto her finger for the first time since 1941. Hope had come home.

For Jesus' followers, hope seemed to die with Jesus on the cross. When Jesus was buried, it felt like hope had been buried. The tomb was sealed, and His friends hid away, leaving hope behind. Hope seemed gone.

But Jesus rose from the grave! When His disciples encountered their risen Savior, an undying and steadfast hope was born in them.

Jesus Christ brings undying hope, a hope that can never be lost or stolen, to every believer. Because Jesus lives, so shall we!

Lord Jesus, I praise You for the undying hope that comes from knowing You as my Savior and Lord!

Week 14   Monday

WALLS OR BRIDGES?

In Christ God was reconciling[a] the world to himself, not counting their trespasses against them, and entrusting to us the message of reconciliation.

2 Corinthians 5:19

Pete Peterson was appointed as the first post-war United States Ambassador to Vietnam, with the goal of working with the Vietnamese government to resolve lingering POW/MIA issues. Pete was uniquely qualified for the position, having been a prisoner of the North Vietnamese army for seven years during the war. His friends asked how he could return to the country where he had been held prisoner.

"I'm not angry," Pete said. "I left my anger at the gates of the prison when I walked out." Pete truly desired to build new bridges of friendship and diplomacy between the two nations.

When we experience deep hurt, our natural response would be to hurt in return or to build walls of separation to protect ourselves from future pain. Neither of those reactions brings reconciliation. They only allow bitterness and isolation to increase.

Followers of Jesus Christ are uniquely qualified to build bridges of peace and reconciliation with those who've hurt us because we have received Jesus Christ's forgiveness for our every transgression against Him. He has built a bridge of reconciliation to us, and in His name, we can build bridges to others when we forgive.

Father, help me to build bridges of reconciliation with others by forgiving them the same way You've forgiven me.

Week 14   Tuesday

PRAY WITHOUT CEASING

Rejoice always, pray without ceasing, give thanks in all circumstances; for this is the will of God in Christ Jesus for you.
1 Thessalonians 5:16-18

Imagine you're traveling with a friend from Florida to California. Being confined with your friend for hours a day over several days would surely result in a good amount of conversation. You would enjoy brief chats and lengthy discussions. There would certainly be occasional interruptions, but so many miles together should produce a steady stream of dialogue.

What if, on the other hand, you make the entire trip in silence? You keep your thoughts to yourself, never even asking a question. That would tell me one of two things – you either do not know your companion, or you don't like them all that much.

Scripture commands us to pray without ceasing. A healthy relationship with Jesus Christ should make us want to talk to Him throughout the day. If you are not talking with Jesus on a regular basis, you either don't know Him, or you really don't love Him very much. God's Word says we are to be in a constant attitude of prayer.

How's your prayer life? Are you talking with Jesus regularly, as you would a good friend? Or do you not really know Jesus, leaving you nothing to talk about?

Father, help me to share my hurts, my needs, as well as my praise and worship with You as I go about my day.

Week 14   Wednesday

MARRED PAINTING

For by grace you have been saved through faith. And this is not your own doing; it is the gift of God, not a result of works, so that no one may boast.

Ephesians 2:8-9

St. Paul's Cathedral houses beautiful paintings by renowned artist, Sir Thomas Thornhill. One day, on the scaffolding from which he worked high above the floor, Sir Thomas paused to admire his work. As he stepped backward, a worker standing near the ceiling quickly took his brush and daubed Thornhill's work with paint. The master stopped short, and angrily cried, "What have you done?"

"I ruined the painting to save the painter," explained the man. "Your next step backward would have killed you."

We can be guilty of presenting to God self-portraits of our best works, religion, morality, and intentions, thinking "God will surely be pleased with me."

Then, to save us from destruction, God strokes His law over our painting, opening our eyes to the fact that we can never be good enough, because we cannot keep the law. We all have sinned and fall short of God's glory.

But God's Son, Jesus Christ, kept the law perfectly and died in our place. When we trust Jesus Christ as Savior and Lord, we trade our "not good enough" for His "good enough." God's salvation is a gift of grace, not of our works.

Father, I thank You that by Your grace, You saved me and gave me the righteousness of Your Son, Jesus Christ.

Week 14 — Thursday

MORNING AND EVENING

It is good to give thanks to the Lord, to sing praises to your name, O Most High; to declare your steadfast love in the morning, and your faithfulness by night.

Psalm 92:1-2

A man wanted to enjoy every tasty bite of his T-bone steak at a fancy restaurant. But he knew it wouldn't be right to gnaw the bone at the table.

He called the waiter over, and asked him to take the bone to the kitchen and put it in a bag as a treat for his dog. The man didn't really have a dog; he just wanted the bone for himself.

The waiter disappeared with the plate. When he returned, he happily offered the guest a full doggie bag, saying, "For you, I took the bones from several plates and packed them for your dog. I hope he enjoys them!"

Do you think that man was interested in eating somebody else's scraps? Of course not.

God is not interested in the scraps of our days. He calls us to a life of daily devotion to Him, making Him our highest priority with the daily discipline of prayer.

Don't give God the leftovers of your time. Make time for prayer a priority in the morning and in the evening. Regularly seeking God in prayer during the prime parts of your day will change your life.

Father, help me to willingly give You the best of my day. Help me to seek You morning and night, and throughout the day in prayer.

Week 14

Friday

DELIVERED

He has delivered us from the domain of darkness and transferred us to the kingdom of His beloved Son.

Colossians 1:13

In our fast paced world, delivery of something to someone somewhere is a daily way of life. Delivery is happening somewhere in our world every minute of every day. Whether your package is transported by FedEx, UPS, or the USPS, delivery is important. It seems to make the world go around.

In the physical world, delivery is the process of moving something or someone from point A to point B.

It's almost the same in the spiritual world. The word "deliver" appears in some form more than five hundred fifty times in the Bible. It would not be unfair to say that the Bible is all about deliverance.

Every Christian has experienced the ultimate form of moving from point A to point B. We've been delivered from the kingdom of darkness into the kingdom God's beloved Son. But that delivery is better than same day; it's instantaneous when we trust Christ!

Have you been delivered? Has God moved you from death to life; from darkness to light; from lost to found? If not, you can be delivered today, and it can happen in an instant when you repent of your sin and call on Jesus to save you. God is in the delivery business!

Father, thank You for delivering me from darkness to Your kingdom when You saved me!

Week 15   Monday

SET FREE FROM THE CHAINS

For freedom Christ has set us free; stand firm therefore, and do not submit again to a yoke of slavery.

Galatians 5:1

A postman nervously walked his new route, aware of the possibility of coming face to face with an unfamiliar dog that might not be happy to see him. His fears were realized when out from behind a house ran a big dog, barking ferociously. Just as the postman jumped back, the dog stopped three feet behind the fence, and plopped down on the front porch.

When the mailman again approached the house, the dog jumped up and repeated his vicious performance. Once again, three feet from the fence, the dog stopped and trotted back toward the porch. Finally the homeowner came to see what the trouble was. When the postman told the story, the man laughed and said, "We just took him off his leash two days ago. Seems he doesn't know he's not chained up anymore!"

Those who trust Jesus Christ for the forgiveness of sin are no longer bound by the chains of keeping rules and regulations to please God. We are no longer slaves to sin and its penalty. Jesus Christ has made us free! We can serve God without fear, knowing that He accepts us in Christ.

In Jesus Christ, your chains have been removed. You are free, so live like it!

Father, help me to live in the freedom You give today.

Week 15   Tuesday

WHO'S THE BOSS?

Bondservants, obey your earthly masters with fear and trembling, with a sincere heart, as you would Christ, not by the way of eye-service, as people-pleasers, but as bondservants of Christ, doing the will of God from the heart, rendering service with a good will as to the Lord and not to man, knowing that whatever good anyone does, this he will receive back from the Lord, whether he is a bondservant or is free.

Ephesians 6:5-8

The average American will work 90,000 hours in a lifetime. That's ten hours a day, seven days a week. No vacation, and no days off for twenty-five years. I'm exhausted just thinking about it.

God made us to work, and He cares about our activity at work. The Bible says we are to obey our earthly masters. If your boss tells you to do something, you are to do it with respect and sincerity, unless it is against God's law, illegal, immoral or unethical.

God also cares about our attitude and ambition at work. We are to always do our best, whether the boss is looking or not. Our highest priority in our work should be to please God. Your ambition in whatever God gives you to do, including your job, should simply be to please Him.

Are you an obedient employee? Are you respectful of your boss and others in authority over you? Do you do your job with sincerity, as to the Lord and not to man? Today, when you go to work, remember, Jesus is your boss!

Father, help me to bring You glory in my work today.

Week 15 — Wednesday

WHO MADE YOU THE BOSS?

Masters, do the same to them, and stop your threatening, knowing that He who is both their Master and yours is in Heaven, and that there is no partiality with Him.

Ephesians 6:9

Everyone is a boss. Even if you don't manage people or run a company, every time you step up to a fast-food counter to order, the server, even if for a very brief moment, works for you. That makes you a boss.

Jesus cares about how you treat those who work for you. Having a greater position, title, or education does not indicate superiority. You may be someone's superior, but that does not mean you are superior. Remember, you have a Master in Heaven that sees no difference in the value between you and those who report to you.

God requires that we treat employees with fairness, patience, generosity, and kindness. Our world is full of people working for unreasonable, demanding, demeaning and unfair bosses. Your workplace is a mission field. Your position as a manager, a boss, or even as a restaurant patron is a platform from which you can show Jesus to those watching.

If your employee comes to your church on Sunday, will what they see in you be the same as what they see on Monday morning? Remember that you have a boss in Heaven. Treat your employees with the same kindness He shows you!

Father, help me to be kind and loving, just as You are, to everyone who works for me.

Week 15   Thursday

YOU LOOK JUST LIKE YOUR DAD!

Therefore be imitators of God, as beloved children.

Ephesians 5:1

Many children look and even sound like their parents. One time when Michele and I were dating, she called our house. My dad answered the phone. Apparently, I sounded just like my dad. She talked to him, thinking it was me. I don't know what all she told him, but she's still embarrassed when she thinks about it!

The Bible says that, as God's beloved children, we are to be like Him. There are two very important ways we can imitate God.

We can imitate God's holiness. The Bible says, "As He who called you is holy, you also be holy in all your conduct." (1 Peter 1:15) We are to forsake immorality, impurity, and greed, and live pure, upright, and generous lives.

We can also imitate God's forgiving love and mercy. We are to "be kind to one another, tenderhearted, forgiving one another, just as God in Christ forgave you." (Ephesians 4:32)

You will never look more like your Father in Heaven than when you forgive like He forgives.

As you yield to God daily and live a life of holiness and forgiveness, you will bear an increasing likeness to your heavenly Father.

---

heavenly Father, help me to imitate You so that when people see me, they see a resemblance to You.

Week 15

Friday

LET YOUR LIGHT SHINE

At one time you were darkness, but now you are light in the Lord. Walk as children of light.

Ephesians 5:8

A little boy attended a church with beautiful stained glass windows that portrayed the lives of Bible characters. Gold plaques told the name of each one – St. Matthew, St. Mark, St. Luke and St. John. When the boy became bored with the sermons, he studied the windows.

One day the boy's Sunday school teacher asked, "What is a saint?" The boy quickly raised his hand and answered, "Saints are the people the light shines through."

In the Bible, darkness represents sin, wickedness, evil, chaos and confusion. Before we are saved, the Bible says we are darkness. Our identity, our heart, our mind, our words, our actions, our future – all darkness. Without Christ, we are darkness.

However, the moment we are saved, God gives us a totally new identity. Now, we are "light in the Lord." Jesus Christ has not only turned on His light in our lives, He wants us to shine His light through us so others can see Him.

Every day we are to walk in the light, seeking Jesus through prayer, and obeying His Word. Let's be people that the light shines through!

Father, thank You that in Christ I am no longer darkness. Help me to walk in Your light today.

Week 16   Monday

UNCLAIMED TREASURE

Let the word of Christ dwell in you richly, teaching and admonishing one another in all wisdom, singing psalms and hymns and spiritual songs, with thankfulness in your hearts to God.

Colossians 3:16

A mother gave her son a brand new Bible as he left for college. "Promise me that you'll read this Bible every day while you're away at school," she said. "It will bless you." He promised that he would.

The young man became so busy at school that he ignored his promise. When he called home to ask for money, His mom replied, "Are you reading your Bible every day? You'll be blessed if you do." Then she said goodbye and hung up.

Every time the young man called to ask for money, his mom's answer was the same. "Read your Bible every day. It will bless you."

Finally, he opened his Bible to read it, and found a sizeable check from his mom. She was right. Reading his Bible blessed him.

You will find great riches when you open God's Word regularly to read and meditate on it. It will teach you, correct you, give you wisdom, move you to thanksgiving, and draw you closer to God's heart in worship. All of these gifts are greater than anything the world gives.

Spend time daily in God's Word. It will make you rich in ways the world never can.

Father, thank You for my Bible. Help me to love Your Word and be changed by it.

Week 16   Tuesday

CLEAN ON THE INSIDE

Have mercy on me, O God, according to your steadfast love; according to your abundant mercy blot out my transgressions. Wash me thoroughly from my iniquity, and cleanse me from my sin!

Psalm 51:1-2

Once, when my wife, Michele, was hosting an event in our home, I offered to wash the windows. I did my very best, using a power washer, to clean the windows upstairs and down.

When I was done, I checked the windows. They were dirty! So, I used window cleaner and extra elbow grease to make sure the windows had no spots on them. I was really frustrated when Michele came to me a little later and said, "The windows are dirty!"

Then I realized that though I had worked hard to clean the windows on the outside, I had done nothing to clean them on the inside.

Cleaning up our lives on the outside doesn't remove the stain of sin on the inside. What can wash away our sin? Nothing but the blood of Jesus.

The Bible says that "the blood of Jesus His Son cleanses us from all sin."(1 John 1:7) There is no stain of sin that the blood of Jesus Christ cannot wash away. When we repent of our sins and confess them to God, "He is faithful and just to forgive us our sins and to cleanse us of all unrighteousness." (1 John 1:9)

Is there sin you need cleansing of today?

Father, thank You for the blood of Jesus that cleanses me from my sin.

Week 16 — Wednesday

FEAR MOVES OUT

For God gave us a spirit not of fear but of power and love and self-control.

2 Timothy 1:7

The great violinist Isaac Stern once made the following observation after seeing a nine-year-old playing the violin amazingly well.

Stern said, "You can't really tell how an artist will be until the teen years, for that is when fear comes. Only then can you see if the person has courage. You can't learn courage until you know fear."

Finding the courage to overcome in the face of fear is an important key to successful living.

The key to walking in power, love, and self-control comes through faith in Jesus Christ. Just having faith does not remedy fear. The object of your faith must be strong enough to faithfully walk you through fearful situations. Jesus is infinitely strong and Jesus is perfectly faithful.

When your faith is in Christ in the middle of a seemingly impossible situation, you are depending on one whose strength, love, power, and faithfulness are perfect. He is greater than anything that can harm you.

You can always trust God's promise: "Fear not, for I am with you; be not dismayed, for I am your God; I will strengthen you, I will help you, I will uphold you with My righteous right hand." (Isaiah 41:10)

Father, give me trust in You that overcomes fear in my life. Thank You for replacing fear with power, love and a sound mind.

Week 16　　　Thursday

CHIPPING STONES OR BUILDING CATHEDRALS

Bondservants, obey your earthly masters with fear and trembling, with a sincere heart, as you would Christ, not by the way of eye-service, as people-pleasers, but as bondservants of Christ, doing the will of God from the heart, rendering service with a good will as to the Lord and not to man, knowing that whatever good anyone does, this he will receive back from the Lord, whether he is a bondservant or is free.

Ephesians 6:5-8

Three stone cutters were working at the site of a new cathedral. A passerby asked each what he was doing. The first man answered, "I'm just chipping away at these stones." The second man said, "I'm just trying to make enough money to get through the day." The third guy's response was much different. "I am building a great cathedral." All three were doing the same job, but one had a vastly different attitude about his work.

Whether you're a floor sweeper or a CEO, whether you make minimum wage or a six figure salary, what matters about your work is your attitude. When you determine that you are going to work to please God more than to please your earthly boss, then God will bring you joy in your work, no matter what your job is.

God is pleased with every person who is doing the job He has given them to do. If He has you working on an assembly line, He is as pleased with you as He is when a pastor preaches a wonderful message. So, whatever He gives you to do, do it for Him!

Father, help me to do Your will from my heart. Thank You that You will reward me for my work.

Week 16

Friday

THE LAST CHAPTER

...the devil who had deceived them was thrown into the lake of fire and sulfur where the beast and the false prophet were, and they will be tormented day and night forever and ever.

Revelation 20:10

A little boy was up late, reading a mystery involving an evil villain. He couldn't stop shivering in dread. When he could stand the suspense no longer, he skipped to the last chapter.

The boy found out that in the end, the villain got what he deserved. Certain of the ending, he was able to relax and read the rest of the book. But now his attitude was different. Every time the villain would plot another evil deed, the boy would smile to himself and say, "If you knew what I know, you wouldn't be so proud and cocky right now." It helps to know how the story ends!

The Bible tells us how the story of good and evil is going to end. Satan will receive his punishment for all eternity. Followers of Jesus will be with Him in Heaven forever. Therefore, we can have great confidence, knowing that Jesus has every situation under His control. He has already won the ultimate victory.

Jesus will reign as King of kings and Lord of lords forever! Satan is already defeated. Therefore, don't live in fear, but in confidence because He that is in you is greater than he who is in the world.

Father, thank You for revealing the end of the story to us in the Bible so we have nothing to fear!

Week 17   Monday

KEEP THE FIRE BURNING

Let marriage be held in honor among all, and let the marriage bed be undefiled, for God will judge the sexually immoral and adulterous.

Hebrews 13:4

I love our fireplace. A fire on a cold night brings warmth and comfort. However, if just a tiny spark jumps out onto the carpet, it can burn the house down.

Intimacy within marriage is like fire in a fireplace; it will bring warmth and comfort to the husband and the wife. Sex is a gift of God to be shared between a husband and a wife within the confines of marriage. Here are some ways to keep the fire burning in your marriage.

Take the time to listen to one another. Real intimacy is not just physical, but also emotional, spiritual, and intellectual. Talk with your spouse daily.

Go on dates weekly. Every married couple needs to date each other. It's key to keeping romance alive and building interest in one another.

Find a time when you can get away with your spouse to rekindle the pleasure of your marriage.

Most importantly, protect your marriage by keeping the fire in the fireplace! Intimacy shared with anyone other than your spouse can burn your marriage and your family, causing deep pain and separation and inviting God's judgment.

Enjoy and protect the intimacy in your marriage. It is a gift from God.

Father, thank You for my spouse. Please bless our marriage today.

Week 17 — Tuesday

ONE MAN AND ONE WOMAN FOR A LIFETIME

So they are no longer two but one flesh. What therefore God has joined together, let not man separate."
Matthew 19:6

Have you ever watched a skillful welder? It's amazing. He takes two pieces of metal, applies extreme heat and bonds them together. When he finishes, there are no longer two disjointed pieces of metal, but one solid, strong, useful piece.

That's what marriage is like. Marriage, established by God in the beginning, is to be a lifetime union of one man and one woman for the protection and development of humankind's deepest physical, psychological, emotional, and spiritual needs. The Bible teaches that when the two are joined at the wedding ceremony and consummate the marriage relationship, they become one flesh, not to be separated until death.

That means you are to love your spouse with the emotion and commitment that comes from the deepest part of you. Second only to your relationship with Jesus Christ, husbands and wives are to be each other's highest love on this earth.

Determine, with God's help, to make your marriage all God intends it to be. Husbands and wives who are faithful to one another and faithful to God bring great glory to the Lord Jesus Christ.

Lord, help our marriage to bring glory to You!

Week 17 — Wednesday

MAINTENANCE

And the rib that the Lord God had taken from the man He made into a woman and brought her to the man. Then the man said, "This at last is bone of my bones and flesh of my flesh; she shall be called Woman, because she was taken out of Man." Therefore a man shall leave his father and his mother and hold fast to his wife, and they shall become one flesh.

Genesis 2:22-24

I've had friends who've built new homes. It's so much fun for them to be able to pick their colors, choose their appliances, add space here and cut space there. If it's a good experience, they end up with the house of their dreams.

But eventually, the roof will need repair, appliances will malfunction, carpets will need cleaning, and walls will need to be painted. Maintenance is always necessary to keep the house functional and enjoyable. No one moves into a new home expecting that it will never need maintenance or repair.

Marriages are a bit like those new houses. They start out fresh and wonderful, but eventually every marriage needs maintenance. When struggles come, a little maintenance helps a marriage operate smoothly again. Occasionally, serious repairs or renovations are needed. Even if a spouse has been unfaithful, with repentance and forgiveness, the marriage can be restored.

God is able to repair broken marriages. You and your spouse are one flesh. Ripping your marriage apart will leave painful wounds for everyone. Instead, humble yourself and bring the ripped pieces of your marriage to Jesus. He is expert at putting broken things back together.

Father, please help marriages that are struggling and broken today.

Week 17 — Thursday

GOING THE DISTANCE

Let all bitterness and wrath and anger and clamor and slander be put away from you, along with all malice. Be kind to one another, tenderhearted, forgiving one another, as God in Christ forgave you. Therefore be imitators of God, as beloved children. And walk in love, as Christ loved us and gave Himself up for us, a fragrant offering and sacrifice to God.

Ephesians 4:31–5:2

When my family moved to Florida several years ago, we loved almost everything about it. The sunny days, the cottony clouds, the beaches, Disney World! There's one thing about Florida, however, that's no fun. Florida is the lightning capital of North America.

Lightning is nothing to play with. Without warning, lightning can strike. It sometimes truly comes "out of the blue." But there are also dark stormy clouds from which lightning strikes, sometimes violently and with great destruction. In Florida, if it thunders, that's a warning to get to a safe place.

Marriages are often struck by lightning. Sometimes it comes out of the blue: a sudden illness, a financial problem, or a miscommunication. Sometimes lightning strikes a marriage from out of storm clouds that have gathered over time as love has grown cold and temptation arises.

When lightning strikes your marriage out of the blue, be quick to respond to your spouse with kindness and forgiveness. When more ominous clouds gather, run to God through prayer, His Word, and godly counsel. That will help your marriage survive even the worst storms.

Father, help me to always be kind and forgiving to my spouse.

Week 17 — Friday

A Prickly Subject

Wives, submit to your own husbands, as to the Lord. For the husband is the head of the wife even as Christ is the head of the church, His body, and is Himself its Savior. Now as the church submits to Christ, so also wives should submit in everything to their husbands.

Ephesians 5:22-24

Heather and Jacob were thrilled to be planning their wedding. As they created the guest list, they poured over names of family and friends they wanted to be there for their big day. Then Jacob said, "We should invite Jesus to the wedding!" And so they added Jesus to their guest list, and issued a formal invitation for Him to attend.

When we invite Jesus Christ into our marriages, He gives us guidelines that are unlike the world's guidelines. God's plan is for wives to submit to their husbands. This instruction may be more misunderstood than any other command in God's Word.

The word "submission," as it is used in God's Word, simply means "to arrange yourself in rank under a leader." It suggests voluntarily yielding to your husband's leadership because of love for him, not because of force. "Submission" never means you are to surrender your safety to an abusive husband. That is not God's plan.

It will glorify God if you will yield to your husband's leadership out of simple obedience to God. God desires to bless your marriage. Obedience to Him always opens the door to His blessing.

Father, thank You that biblical submission to my husband is designed to bless me, not to hurt me.

Week 18   Monday

LOVE AND MARRIAGE

Husbands, love your wives, as Christ loved the church and gave Himself up for her, that He might sanctify her, having cleansed her by the washing of water with the Word, so that He might present the church to Himself in splendor, without spot or wrinkle or any such thing, that she might be holy and without blemish.

Ephesians 5:25-27

In 1955, Frank Sinatra recorded the hit song, "Love and Marriage." The catchy lyrics say, "Love and marriage, love and marriage, go together like a horse and carriage." The thought of a horse and carriage stirs visions of romance, unless you envision a scene from an old western where the hitch breaks, the horse gallops away and the carriage goes careening out of control, headed for a rocky cliff. In other words, if love has left a marriage, then the marriage is headed for the rocks.

Every marriage can use more love. You can ruin a dessert with too much sugar, but you'll never mess up a marriage with more love. God specifically commands husbands to love their wives. The standard against which that love is measured is the sacrificial love Christ has for the church.

The Bible says that a husband's love for his wife will sanctify her, allowing her to become all that God has created her to be. A husband's love is never to be demanding or demeaning. It is to be safe and ,encouraging, allowing his wife to grow physically, spiritually and emotionally. Husbands, God will bless your marriage when you love your wife.

Father, help me to love my wife with Your kind of love.

Week 18   Tuesday

JUST WHAT YOU'RE LOOKING FOR

He came to His own, and His own people did not receive Him. But to all who did receive Him, who believed in His name, He gave the right to become children of God.

John 1:11-12

Here's a little experiment you can try that will teach you about your focus and attention: wherever you are, look around and identify five things that are blue. When you're looking for "blue," it jumps out: a book, a car, a carpet, a piece of clothing.

Have you ever noticed that when you get a new car, you begin to see others like it everywhere you go? Why is that? Well, we all tend to find what we're looking for.

When Jesus came to earth, many didn't recognize Him as the promised Messiah because He wasn't exactly what they were looking for.

You will always see Jesus when you are looking for Him. The first place to look is in God's Word, the Bible. The Bible tells the story of Jesus, shows us how to follow Jesus, and allows Jesus to speak to us. Look for Jesus in the body of Christ, His Church. Jesus shows Himself and encourages us through His followers. Then look for Jesus in your life every day. Keep your eyes and ears open for the Holy Spirit to show you opportunities to serve Christ.

If you don't see Jesus, chances are very good that you're just not looking!

Lord Jesus, help me to see You and Your activity around me today.

Week 18   Wednesday

A New Commandment

A new commandment I give to you, that you love one another:
just as I have loved you, you also are to love one another. By
this all people will know that you are My disciples, if you have
love for one another."

John 13:34-35

Have you ever seen a little girl come shuffling out of her parents' bedroom dressed like her mom? She trips along in mom's high heels and wags a purse on her tiny arm, and may have a smear of lipstick to top it off. It's a great photo op, and creates pride in a parent's heart when they see their child wanting to be just like them.

Jesus commands us to be like Him by loving other people like He loves us. Christ's love is a costly love, a sacrificial love. Here are some practical ways of loving others the way Jesus loves us.

> Listen to each other in a way that really hears.
>
> Spend time with your spouse, kids, and friends.
>
> Look for opportunities to encourage, affirm, and appreciate those you love.
>
> Laugh together! It relieves stress and grows affection for one another.
>
> Accept those closest to you, no matter what. They need to be assured that no mistake they can make will ever sever them from your love.

How can you love people practically today? You will never look more like Jesus than when you love others the way He loves.

Father, help me to sacrificially love others as You do.

Week 18 — Thursday

THE TASTE OF PRAISE

He put a new song in my mouth, a song of praise to our God. Many will see and fear, and put their trust in the Lord.

Psalm 40:3

Our family enjoys a big family breakfast every Saturday. Sometimes we have sausage and pancakes with real maple syrup. And, of course, we drink Florida orange juice with our meal.

Sometimes I make a strategic breakfast mistake. I'll take a bite of my pancake, and then drink the orange juice. As a result, the orange juice, which is normally very sweet, tastes incredibly sour.

In Africa, there is a fruit called the "taste berry." The berry rewires the way the palate perceives sour flavors, rendering lemons as sweet as candy. Eating one of those before my pancake and juice breakfast might be just the trick to help me enjoy my OJ with pancakes.

Praise is like a spiritual taste berry. When we offer praise to the Lord, the sourness we feel over bitter and unpleasant circumstances is transformed.

That's why it's so important to come together with other believers for worship each week. We sweeten each other's lives through corporate praise in the church. In the same way, it is vital to make praise a part of your personal prayer time each day.

Every day, spend some time praising the Lord. It will make your day a lot sweeter!

Lord, I praise You today for Your goodness and kindness!

Week 18   Friday

JUST SAY "NO"

But sexual immorality and all impurity or covetousness must not even be named among you, as is proper among saints.

Ephesians 5:3

Nancy Reagan was responsible for a very successful anti-drug campaign during her husband's presidency. It was called "Just Say No." The name for her cause was chosen when a little girl raised her hand during a meeting and asked, "Mrs. Reagan, what do you do if somebody offers you drugs?"

"Well," Mrs. Reagan responded, "you just say 'no.' "

In order for followers of Jesus Christ to walk in God's love, we must say "no" to ungodliness. This passage talks about three categories of sin we are to reject.

We are to reject sexual immorality. This includes sex before marriage, sex outside of the marriage, homosexuality, and pornography.

We are to say "no" to impurity, specifically in our speech. Obscenity, foolish talk, and dirty jokes – telling them and listening to them) are out of place for a child of God.

We are to say "no" to covetousness. Greed is a form of idolatry, causing us to put money and possessions in a place only God deserves to be as the object of all of our affection.

When you are tempted to be like the world, you can just say "no" through the power of the Holy Spirit of God living in you.

Father, help me to live a pure and godly life today.

Week 19   Monday

WE ARE JESUS' BODY

Now you are the body of Christ and individually members of it.
1 Corinthians 12:27

Years ago, *Reader's Digest* published a series of articles called the "I Am Joe's ..." articles. Each article was written in the voice of a human organ – the heart, the liver, etc. – to educate the reader about its purpose in the body and how to best care for it. It also emphasized the necessity of each part for the proper function of the whole body.

The Bible says that we are members of the body of Christ. God has put together each church fellowship with the right parts to fulfill God's purpose for that congregation.

For the church body to be healthy, all of its members must be spiritually healthy. This happens when each member spends time daily in God's Word and prayer, and remains strongly connected to the local church body where we exercise our faith by obeying and serving the Lord Jesus Christ together.

Praise the Lord that He loves you so much that He has made you part of His body. Today, look for ways to serve Him as a member of His body, the church.

Father, thank You for giving me gifts and talents to use for Your service.

Week 19   Tuesday

PRIORITIES

Do not lay up for yourselves treasures on earth, where moth and rust destroy and where thieves break in and steal, but lay up for yourselves treasures in Heaven, where neither moth nor rust destroys and where thieves do not break in and steal. For where your treasure is, there your heart will be also.

Matthew 6:19-21

Urban legend says that several years ago burglars broke into a large department store at night. They stole nothing, nor damaged any property. Instead, they simply swapped price tags on items throughout the store. When they were finished, a $395 camera was now only $5, the price of a box of film. A $7 towel was now $50, the price of a towel rack. And so it went in every department.

In the morning, it was some time before anyone noticed what had happened. Customers bagged great deals because no one realized that the price tags had been swapped.

We will always be tempted to inflate the value of unimportant things, while devaluing what is very important. Our first priority is to seek God's kingdom and pursue His glory in our jobs, at school, in our marriages, in the marketplace, and in our citizenship. Nothing in our lives should be done apart from seeking God's kingdom and His glory.

God's Word warns us against getting our priorities confused. Where is your treasure? What is your focus? Who is your master? When Jesus Christ is your highest priority, everything else will maintain its correct value.

Lord Jesus, help me to make Your priorities my priorities.

Week 19 — Wednesday

FOR EXAMPLE...

Jesus said: "For I have given you an example, that you also should do just as I have done to you."

John 13:15

It's been said that a pint of example is worth a gallon of advice.

Imagine teaching a child to tie his shoes using words alone. You might say: "Take the laces and cross them in the opposite directions on top of your shoe. Then pull one of them underneath. Now pull on the ends of both strings and tighten the knot you just made. Now, take the string on the left and make a loop with it...." This could get really frustrating really fast.

It goes much better when we say, *"Here, let me show you..."*

Whose example are you following? The most important person whose example we should follow is Jesus. He came to earth to say, "Here, let me show you." To see Jesus's example, it's as simple as opening your Bible.

There are also contemporary role models to follow as you live your life for Christ. Find others who walk with Him faithfully, and follow their example. They will be a great encouragement to you.

Then consider this. Who is following your example? Will following your example lead them toward God or away from Him?

Father, help me to be a Christ-like example to all who are watching me.

Week 19   Thursday

RIGHT WORD, RIGHT PLACE

And you, who were dead in your trespasses and the uncircumcision of your flesh, God made alive together with Him, having forgiven us all our trespasses.

Colossians 2:13

A journalism professor created a sentence which can have eight completely different meanings depending on the placement of the word "only." Here's the sentence:

I hit him in the eye yesterday. Consider the variations:

    Only I hit him in the eye yesterday.

    I *only* hit him in the eye yesterday.

    I hit *only* him in the eye yesterday.

    I hit him *only* in the eye yesterday.

    I hit him in the eye *only* yesterday.

    I hit him in the eye yesterday *only*.

As you can see, just one little word, in the right place, can make a big difference.

We deserve God's punishment for every sin we commit. But there's a single word that can make all the difference in your standing with God. That word is *forgiven.*

Every person who trusts Jesus Christ as Savior is forgiven! When we call on Jesus to save us, He forgives all of our sins, past, present, and future. Today, you can stand in freedom and joy because of one simple word made possible by the awesome work of Jesus when He died on the cross. You have been forgiven!

Father, I thank You for Your undeserved forgiveness for my sin!

Week 19

Friday

TRUST

Therefore I tell you, do not be anxious about your life, what you will eat or what you will drink, nor about your body, what you will put on. Is not life more than food, and the body more than clothing? Look at the birds of the air: they neither sow nor reap nor gather into barns, and yet your heavenly Father feeds them. Are you not of more value than they?

Matthew 6:25-26

Recently I was out walking in my yard to see how the grass was coming in. I was happy to see a good portion of thick, lush grass. But there were several spots where something else was growing. Weeds.

Have you noticed that weeds will grow where grass won't? Weeds can grow anywhere, but we especially notice them where they're not wanted. That's part of the Adamic curse; it just happens that way.

I did notice that where the thick, healthy grass grew there was no room for weeds to grow. The healthy grass crowded them out.

Worry is like a weed. It springs up and takes over where there is no faith to crowd it out. But when your life is filled with trust in God, when your faith in Him and His promises is growing and healthy, worry will decrease. But where trust in God is decreasing, worries will fill that space like weeds taking over a barren lawn.

We must combat worry by sowing seeds of faith in God and His promises. When faith takes over, doubts must flee. God is greater than all of the worries that we face.

Father, thank You that You are greater than all my worries.

Week 20   Monday

IT'S GOOD TO BE KING

They will make war on the Lamb, and the Lamb will conquer them, for He is Lord of lords and King of kings, and those with Him are called and chosen and faithful.

Revelation 17:14

Some frogs became discontent with their way of life, and thought they should have a mighty ruler. So they asked for a king. Suddenly, a large log fell across the water, and a sonorous voice from above said, "Behold your king!"

The frogs saw that the log did not move, and they began to climb on it. This was no king. He did nothing. So they asked for a real king.

A large stork appeared. Again the voice from above proclaimed, "Behold your king!" The stork began eating the frogs. The frogs cried out in terror, asking for the king to be taken away. The voice replied: "You got what you asked for. Now you must face the consequences."

Many kings compete for the throne of our lives. The kings of pleasure, money, power, position, education, entertainment – any king other than Jesus Christ – will always leave us wanting and without promise of better things. These kings will always take more than their share.

Jesus Christ is the King over all kings. His reign brings hope, peace, love, and joy. Let Jesus rule your life today. It's good to have that kind of king.

Lord Jesus, You are my Lord and my King. Help me to please You with my life.

Week 20   Tuesday

LIGHT IN THE LORD

For at one time you were darkness, but now you are light in the Lord. Walk as children of light, (for the fruit of light is found in all that is good and right and true), and try to discern what is pleasing to the Lord.

Ephesians 5: 8-10

Not long ago, Michele and I replaced burned-out bulbs in a light fixture in our home with new bulbs. When we turned the switch on, the two new bulbs were not as bright as the old ones. We then realized we had replaced 100-watt bulbs with 40-watt bulbs. We didn't want 40-watt light; we wanted 100-watt light. So back to the store we went for the proper bulbs.

When you have the capacity to be a 100-watt Christian, are you willing to settle for shining a 40-watt light for Jesus?

We shine brightest when we are producing the fruit of the light: all that is good, and right and true. We are to live daily as children of light, learning to live in a way that is pleasing to the Lord.

Light is required to shine in the darkness and show the way to Jesus. People who need Jesus need a strong light to show them the way.

By the way, light bulbs don't shine their light unless they are connected to the power source. We are only light when we are in the Lord. Today, stay connected to Jesus and let Him shine His light through you.

Lord Jesus, thank You that when I walk with You I have all the light I need.

Week 20 — Wednesday

BATTLEGROUND

Finally, be strong in the Lord and in the strength of His might. Put on the whole armor of God, that you may be able to stand against the schemes of the devil. For we do not wrestle against flesh and blood, but against the rulers, against the authorities, against the cosmic powers over this present darkness, against the spiritual forces of evil in the heavenly places. Therefore take up the whole armor of God, that you may be able to withstand in the evil day, and having done all, to stand firm.

Ephesians 6:10-13

A boxer was being pummeled in the ring by his opponent. Blow after blow from his adversary left him with a bloody nose, swollen eyes, and an enormous amount of pain. His trainer tried to encourage him between rounds, telling him, "You're doing great, Fred. That bum is barely touching you."

The weary boxer responded, "Then you better keep your eye on the referee because somebody out there is killing me!" No amount of smooth talk could camouflage the reality of the battle in which this fighter was engaged.

You and I are engaged in a real battle. Spiritual warfare is a reality that believers face every day. When God saved you, He did not put you on a playground; He put you on a battleground.

However, don't be discouraged. Our enemy, Satan, witnessed his defeat when Jesus offered Himself up on the cross for our sin and was raised from the dead. Be strong in the Lord and in the power of His might! Christ's victory is your victory. Cling to Him, and He will strengthen you to fight the good fight, and to remain faithful and strong to the end.

Father, You are stronger than all my enemies. Help me to stand and be faithful today.

Week 20   Thursday

THE BEST LAID PLANS

Come now, you who say, "Today or tomorrow we will go into such and such a town and spend a year there and trade and make a profit"— yet you do not know what tomorrow will bring. What is your life? For you are a mist that appears for a little time and then vanishes. Instead you ought to say, "If the Lord wills, we will live and do this or that." As it is, you boast in your arrogance. All such boasting is evil.

James 4:13-16

A milkmaid on her way to the farmhouse carried a pail of milk on her head.

As she walked, she began to daydream of how she would get cream from the milk, which she would churn into butter, which she would sell at the market, which would give her money to buy eggs, which would produce chickens, which she could sell to buy a beautiful dress to wear to the dance.

Thinking about the dance, she tossed her head grandly, causing the pail to tip over, spilling all of the milk, and spoiling her hopeful dream.

When she told her mother what had happened, her mother said, "Ah, my child, you should not have counted your chickens before they were hatched." And thus came about the famous expression that warns us of unwisely acting on future aspirations before they come to fruition.

Making plans is a necessary part of life. But presuming to make our own plans without leaving God in charge of our appointment book is not only foolish, but prideful and sinful.

It's fine to pencil plans into your calendar, but realize that God has editing rights! Today, make sure all your plans are surrendered to Jesus.

Lord, by faith I surrender all my plans to You.

Week 20

Friday

OVEREXPOSURE

Take no part in the unfruitful works of darkness, but instead expose them. For it is shameful even to speak of the things that they do in secret. But when anything is exposed by the light, it becomes visible.

Ephesians 5:11-13

I know of a carpet cleaning company that offers a special cleaning service for homes with pets. The homeowner often responds, "We don't need that. Our pet is housebroken, and when there's mess, we get it clean."

That's when the technician darkens the room, and turns on a powerful black-light that causes the crystals formed by animal "dribbles" to glow brightly. To the horror of the homeowner, every drop instantly becomes visible, not only on the carpet, but on the walls, the drapes, and the furniture. That's all it takes to sell the special service to the customer.

God's light exposes our sins. It brings to light things we'd rather not think about. The stains of our sin are real, and no amount of our own scrubbing can remove them.

However, Jesus' stain removal service is 100% guaranteed. You may fear that your mess is so disgusting that Jesus would never want to touch it. But He wants to clean up our worst sin and completely remove its stain.

Has Jesus exposed a sin you need to let Him clean up? Don't stay in darkness. Instead, let Him clean up everything that is exposed by His light.

Lord, as You expose the sin in my life, help me to confess and let You cleanse me of it.

Week 21   Monday

LEARN TO DISCERN

Beware of false prophets, who come to you in sheep's clothing but inwardly are ravenous wolves.

Matthew 7:15

A sinister wolf disguised his appearance to secure food more easily. Wrapped in the fleece of a sheep, he grazed with the flock unnoticed. At the end of the day, the shepherd secured the sheep inside the pen for the evening and retired. Then the wolf began to stalk his prey. The shepherd returned unexpectedly to the fold, and found the wolf taking aim at an unsuspecting sheep. The shepherd killed him instantly.

False doctrine may seem harmless. False teachers often have winning personalities and deliver messages with charm. However, wolves in sheep's clothing always have the intention of destroying God's flock.

Every preacher and Bible teacher must line up with only one standard – God's Word. Any teaching that deviates even slightly from the Bible must be rejected. Believers must be thoroughly familiar with God's Word in order to recognize false teachers.

Leaders who bear the fruit of godliness and adhere to the Word of God show they come from God. Those whose lives are filled with hypocrisy and inconsistency show they don't come from God.

Don't be fooled by wolves in sheep's clothing. Instead, pray to be able to recognize falsehood when it appears.

Father, help me to recognize false doctrine and only listen to Your truth.

Week 21   Tuesday

JUDGE NOT

Judge not, that you be not judged. For with the judgment you pronounce you will be judged, and with the measure you use it will be measured to you. Why do you see the speck that is in your brother's eye, but do not notice the log that is in your own eye? Or how can you say to your brother, 'Let me take the speck out of your eye,' when there is the log in your own eye? You hypocrite, first take the log out of your own eye, and then you will see clearly to take the speck out of your brother's eye.

Matthew 7:1-5

Every day, Margaret battled with her little Yorkshire terrier, Patches. She would hold the squirming dog tightly, and try to force a dose of castor oil down his throat. It was all for his own good.

One day, Patches managed to escape, and overturned the bottle of oil. When a frustrated Margaret came to mop up the mess, she found Patches happily licking up the oil. Then Margaret realized that Patches didn't hate castor oil at all. He just hated having it forced down his throat.

None of us meets God's standard of holiness. None is perfect, nor will we be, until we are in Heaven with Jesus. We're often more interested in judging people than in loving them and sharing the gospel of Jesus with them.

We need to rightly judge ourselves to make sure we are right with God? Then, when we have clean hands and a pure heart, let us lovingly call others to obey Jesus in a spirit of gentleness.

The gospel, not our judgment of others, is the power of God to save. Let us love people, and leave them with the gospel.

Father, help me pour the gospel out for people instead of pouring judgment on them.

102

Week 21 — Wednesday

SECRET WEAPON

In all circumstances take up the shield of faith, with which you can extinguish all the flaming darts of the evil one...
Ephesians 6:16

A tale is told of the devil holding a yard sale to sell his arsenal of weapons. The tables were piled with missiles labeled lust, lies, drugs, alcohol, pornography, adultery, and rebellion. Many people stopped by to see if they wanted to buy anything from Satan's yard sale.

One weapon was obviously more used and worn than the others. It was priced ten times higher than the other weapons. A shopper asked the devil, "What is this weapon? And why do you want so much for it?"

Satan replied, "That's my favorite. It's called 'Discouragement.' When the other weapons don't work, or when I can't tempt a person or even deceive them, then I pull out good old 'Discouragement.' It renders them useless almost one hundred percent of time." Then he said, "Most people don't even know it belongs to me."

Discouragement is one of Satan's flaming darts. It's very effective in stealing joy, killing effectiveness, and destroying hope.

Are you discouraged today? Hold up your shield of faith! Even the fiery darts of discouragement will be extinguished as you hold to the promises of God and trust in the overcoming power of Jesus.

Father, help me to hold up the shield of faith You have given me when I am discouraged.

Week 21　　　Thursday

ALL THINGS

And we know that for those who love God all things work together for good, for those who are called according to His purpose.

Romans 8:28

Hien Pham, a Vietnamese Christian who served as a translator for Americans during the war in Vietnam, was imprisoned when the war was over for aiding the enemy. An endless barrage of Communist propaganda in the prison eventually shook his faith in Christ.

After some time, Hien was assigned to latrine duty. As he cleaned a toilet, he spied a piece of paper with English words. He washed it off and slipped it into his pocket. That night as other prisoners slept, Hien pulled out the paper and saw at the top, "Romans, Chapter 8."

Hien realized that God had supernaturally brought His Word just when he had decided to turn from his faith. He sought God for forgiveness and restoration, and faithfully served God throughout his time in prison.

Even in the most horrible situation, God works all things for good for those who are His.

What terrible circumstance are you in? A broken marriage? Financial ruin? Job loss? Rebellious children? Cancer? The death of a loved one? Life is full of things that can cause our hearts to break and threaten our peace.

Even when you cannot see Him, you can trust God. He will never forget you!

Father, I choose to trust You today, even if I can't see You. Thank You for Your faithfulness.

Week 21   Friday

THE LION'S SHARE

He is the image of the invisible God, the firstborn of all creation.
For by Him all things were created, in Heaven and on earth,
visible and invisible, whether thrones or dominions or rulers or
authorities—all things were created through Him and for Him.
And He is before all things, and in Him all things hold together.
And He is the head of the body, the church. He is the beginning,
the firstborn from the dead, that in everything He might be
preeminent.

Colossians 1:15-18

A lion, a fox, and a donkey went hunting together. When the donkey divided their catch into three equal portions, the angry lion pounced on the poor donkey and ate him. With great wisdom, the fox put most everything in one large pile, and left just a tiny bit in a much smaller pile. She then invited the lion to choose his share.

When the lion asked what prompted her to share like that, the fox replied, "The donkey's bad example."

That story points to a much deeper truth: Jesus Christ, the lion of Judah, does not ask for the "lion's share" of your life. He wants your life.

Jesus Christ is above everything. He is God. He is the creator of everything we can see and everything we can't see. He holds everything together. He holds you together. He alone deserves the highest place in your life.

Have you bowed in surrender before Jesus Christ, the King of kings and Lord of lords? Jesus is all-powerful and preeminent, but He is also loving and merciful. You can entrust your whole life to Him.

Lord Jesus, You are the King of my life. Help me to daily
surrender all I am and have to You.

Week 22 — Monday

UNLIMITED ACCESS

Ask, and it will be given to you; seek, and you will find; knock, and it will be opened to you. For everyone who asks receives, and the one who seeks finds, and to the one who knocks it will be opened.

Matthew 7:7-8

Several years ago, the President of Indonesia met with a group of his country's farmers to listen to their concerns over issues they were experiencing with the government.

He wanted the farmers to know he was listening and desired to respond to their complaints. So, he gave his personal cellphone number to them and invited them to call him any time to voice their concerns. It seemed like a good idea at the time.

Soon, the number was available around the world. The president's phone crashed from the crushing call volume. Not only was he unable to respond to most of the messages he received, he never received most of what was sent to him.

God is unlimited in His ability to hear every prayer uttered to Him through Christ. When God's children cry out to Him, He hears. He will never be out of range. He will never send you to voicemail. He will never be too busy to hear.

God not only hears our prayers, He answers every prayer. Everyone who asks receives. Everyone who seeks finds. He opens the door to everyone who knocks. You call out to God, and He will answer.

Father, thank You for hearing and answering my prayers.

Week 22 — Tuesday

LOVE WINS THE DAY

And He said to him, "You shall love the Lord your God with all your heart and with all your soul and with all your mind. This is the great and first commandment. And a second is like it: You shall love your neighbor as yourself. On these two commandments depend all the Law and the Prophets."

Matthew 22:37-40

The North Wind and the Sun argued over which was stronger. When a traveler came along wrapped in a warm cloak, they agreed that the one who first succeeded in making the traveler remove his cloak would be declared the stronger of the two.

The North Wind blew as hard as he could. The traveler wound his cloak more tightly around him. Finally, the North Wind gave up his attempt. Then the Sun shined out warmly. Immediately the traveler removed his cloak. The North Wind was obliged to confess that the Sun was the stronger of the two.

Most people are moved more by the warmth of encouragement and love than by the harshness of cold criticism. God's Word says, "Owe no one anything, except to love each other, for the one who loves another has fulfilled the law." (Romans 13:8)

The law of God reveals His heart, which is filled with total, all-out love for mankind.

Passionately loving Christ creates in us His kind of love for others. When we have radical love for God and the people He has created, we fulfill the purpose that Jesus has for us.

Lord, help me to love You with all my heart, and help me to love other people.

Week 22　Wednesday

IS THERE A BEATING HEART?

I will sprinkle clean water on you, and you shall be clean from all your uncleannesses, and from all your idols I will cleanse you. And I will give you a new heart, and a new spirit I will put within you. And I will remove the heart of stone from your flesh and give you a heart of flesh. And I will put My Spirit within you, and cause you to walk in My statutes and be careful to obey My rules.

Ezekiel 36:25-27

Bill was an overweight, frenetic businessman when his body rebelled against his lifestyle. His heart failed, requiring a transplant for Bill to live.

Bill's new heart came from an incredibly fit and extremely athletic thirty-six-year-old man who had been killed in an accident. It would have been almost irreverent to continue in the lifestyle that almost killed Bill after receiving such a wonderful, healthy, new heart.

Bill radically changed his life to match his new heart, even becoming an athlete himself. When asked about his new-found passion, Bill said, "Every day I thank God for my donor. I changed my life to honor him."

When we receive Jesus Christ as Savior and Lord, He gives us a brand new heart. The Holy Spirit of God lives in our new heart. Our priorities should reflect His character.

Are you living to bring honor and glory to Jesus Christ? Are you striving to keep the commandments of Jesus? Are you building up treasure on earth or in Heaven? Are you taking the gospel to the lost? Let your new heart match the priorities of the One who gave it to you!

Father, help me to live today to honor You in everything I do.

108

Week 22   Thursday

YOUR SPIRITUAL SENSES

That which was from the beginning, which we have heard, which we have seen with our eyes, which we looked upon and have touched with our hands, concerning the Word of life ... we proclaim also to you, so that you too may have fellowship with us; and indeed our fellowship is with the Father and with His Son Jesus Christ.

1 John 1:1-3

Our senses of sight, smell, hearing, tasting, and touching help us interpret our world.

Jesus' followers saw, touched, and heard Jesus. They tasted His sacrifice at the Last Supper. They experienced the aroma of His presence when He was anointed with the costly perfume of worship.

Although Jesus is no longer physically with us, God still allows us to experience Him with our spiritual senses. The Lord connects with us through spiritual sight. "As we look not to the things that are seen but to the things that are unseen." (2 Corinthians 4:18)

God connects with us through spiritual hearing. "My sheep hear My voice..." (John 10:27) God connects with our sense of smell. "Through us (God) spreads the fragrance of the knowledge of Him everywhere." (2 Corinthians 2:14) The Lord even connects through our sense of taste. "Oh, taste and see that the Lord is good!" (Psalm 34:8)

Actively listening to God through His Word, watching for His activity around us, lifting a fragrant offering of worship, and tasting His goodness will heighten our awareness of Christ's presence and His work in us as we seek Him each day.

Father, help me to be aware of Your work around me today. Help me to hear and see You in my life.

Week 22   Friday

JURISDICTION

And Jesus came and said to them, "All authority in Heaven and on earth has been given to Me. Go therefore and make disciples of all nations, baptizing them in the name of the Father and of the Son and of the Holy Spirit.

Matthew 28:18-19

As a boy, I loved to watch "The Dukes of Hazzard." It featured the comical Sheriff Rosco P. Coltrane, who was continually in "hot pursuit" of his nemeses, Bo and Luke Duke. They outran and outsmarted him every time.

Dust flew, engines whined, and tires screeched as the sheriff wildly chased the Duke boys across Hazzard county. As soon as Bo and Luke entered the next county, they skidded to a stop, pulled themselves through the car windows, and calmly waited for the frustrated sheriff to brake to a halt on the other side. Sheriff Coltrane couldn't arrest them, and he couldn't keep chasing them. Why? Because once they were outside Hazzard County, Bo and Luke were out of Rosco's jurisdiction.

No part of this universe exceeds the jurisdiction of Jesus Christ. He has all authority on this earth and beyond. His authority empowers our mission to take the gospel to the ends of the earth. There are no boundaries as we go in His name.

As we obey Christ, nothing can stand against us, because nothing can stand against Him! Let's exercise that authority today as we obey His commands and take His gospel to the world.

Father, thank You that You rule over everything that affects my life today.

Week 23   Monday

REDEEMING YOUR PAST

Brothers, I do not consider that I have made it my own. But one thing I do: forgetting what lies behind and straining forward to what lies ahead, I press on toward the goal for the prize of the upward call of God in Christ Jesus.

Philippians 3:13-14

Concerned that he was losing his memory, a man went to his doctor for advice. After examining him, the doctor said: "We can't help your memory without impairing your eyesight. You must choose. Do you want to see or to remember?"

The man wryly answered, "I'd rather see where I am going than remember where I've been!"

All of us have sin, regret, and sorrow from past sins that we'd like to forget. For some, memories of our past become a club the devil uses to beat us down.

Focusing on past failures keeps us from trusting God. God's Word reminds us to leave the past behind and move ahead to what He has for us.

You can't drive down the highway continually looking in your rearview mirror. Neither can you live the Christian life by constantly looking to the past. God is able to redeem the regrets, mistakes, and sins of our past and use them to bring glory to Himself.

When we receive forgiveness from our sin through the blood of Jesus Christ, God tosses our sin into the sea of forgetfulness. He does not dwell on your forgiven sins. Why should you?

Father, thank You so much that You forgive the sins and redeem the mistakes of my past.

Week 23   Tuesday

THE POWER OF FAILURE

For the sake of Christ, then, I am content with weaknesses, insults, hardships, persecutions, and calamities. For when I am weak, then I am strong.

2 Corinthians 12:10

Recounting a business disaster early in his career, Walt Disney said: "I think it's important to have a good, hard failure when you're young." Disney cherished his failures because of lessons learned, and because it created an increased appreciation for success

We all know failure is hard. Few of us think about failure being good. Our failures and weaknesses, when surrendered to God, become very effective tools used by Him to conform us to the image of His Son, Jesus Christ.

The greatest benefit of failure is that it chips away at our self-sufficiency, causing us to bind ourselves more securely to Jesus. The apostle Paul experienced this. Though he asked God on three occasions to remove a difficult physical issue from him, a life without weakness was not God's plan for Paul.

Instead, God taught Paul that His grace was enough to strengthen Paul despite his limitations, and that His amazing power was best appropriated in Paul's life through his weakness.

Today, let your weaknesses and failures move you toward trusting God more completely. He'll work in your weakness to show Himself strong.

Lord, thank You for using my failures to mold and shape me for Your purposes.

Week 23 — Wednesday

STOPPED FOR ENCOURAGEMENT

For whatever was written in former days was written for our instruction, that through endurance and through the encouragement of the Scriptures we might have hope.

Romans 15:4

A young woman anxiously awaited as a police officer approached her car, ticket pad in hand. Imagine her relief with the officer smiled and handed her a ticket that read, "Your driving is great, and we appreciate it!" With it, he handed her two dollars. This was part of the city's effort to encourage safe drivers, and it worked!

God is our greatest encourager. He blesses us with comfort, friendship, and help. The Bible says that God comforts us in every hardship so we can comfort others in the same way He comforts us (2 Corinthians 1:3-4).

Jesus is our friend. (John 15:15) Just think of how comforting it is to know your friend is standing with you through thick and thin. A friend loves at all times. Jesus is that friend to us.

The Holy Spirit is our Helper. (John 14:16-17) He is with us forever. He dwells in us. If you ever feel alone, remember the Holy Spirit is with you every moment.

God's endless encouragement is available to you at all times as He speaks to you through His Word and through prayer. If you're not encouraged, maybe you're not listening!

Father, thank you for Your constant encouragement through Your Word and the Holy Spirit living in me.

Week 23   Thursday

A FLY IN THE OINTMENT

You have heard that it was said, "You shall love your neighbor and hate your enemy." But I say to you, love your enemies and pray for those who persecute you ...

Matthew 5:43-44

A bald man sat to rest after working hard on a hot summer's day. As soon as he relaxed, a fly flew close and buzzed about his shiny head. A few times, the fly even bit him.

Irritated, the man aimed a blow at the pesky little enemy. He missed the fly, but swatted his own head.

Again and again the fly buzzed around the man's head to torment him. Again and again, the frustrated man swatted and missed, leaving red marks all over his head.

The moral of the story? When you pay undue attention to your enemies, you only hurt yourself.

Most of us encounter personal enemies from time to time. People will try to hurt us, put us down, or simply annoy us with their attitudes and words.

What do we do with those who stand against us? Jesus commands us to love our enemies. We are to bless them, do them good, and pray for those who would try to harm us.

Consider the people who are "flies in the ointment" of your life. What can you do today to respond to them sincerely with the love and grace of Jesus Christ?

Father, please help me to respond with kindness to every person who rubs me the wrong way today!

Week 23

HE IS WORTHY

Worthy is the Lamb who was slain, to receive power and wealth and wisdom and might and honor and glory and blessing!
Revelation 5:11-12

A gifted violinist attempted to purchase a rare Stradivarius violin from an old gentleman who insisted it was not for sale. The prospective buyer asked, "May I just touch it?"

The old man permitted the younger musician to hold the instrument and then nodded in agreement that he should play it. The violinist tenderly tuned the instrument, positioned it under his chin, and drew the bow across the strings. The music that came from the Stradivarius evoked magical and moving sounds that brought the violin's owner to tears.

When the violinist attempted to give the instrument back to its owner, he would not accept it. The old man said, "It is not for sale, but it is yours. You alone are worthy of it!"

One day, all believers from all the ages will be gathered together in Heaven, where we will worship Jesus alone. He, alone, is worthy of all worship and praise for all eternity.

That will be a glorious time. But don't wait for Heaven to worship. Don't wait for Sunday to worship! Jesus Christ is worthy of our worship every day. Take a few moments to worship Jesus today. It will bless you, and it will bless our Lord!

Father, I worship You today. You are an awesome God!

Week 24   Monday

THE STREAM OF GOD'S BLESSING

Blessed is the man who walks not in the counsel of the wicked, nor stands in the way of sinners, nor sits in the seat of scoffers; but his delight is in the law of the Lord, and on His law he meditates day and night.

Psalm 1:1-2

In the hot summer, nothing beats a lazy trip down the river in a tube. I've learned there's a trick to really enjoying the tubing experience, and that is to stay where the water moves freely downstream.

Many things can keep you from enjoying the ride. If you're not careful, you can get stuck on the rocks, stall in an eddy, or drift too close to the bank. Any of those can keep you from moving down the river. But, if you remain in the moving stream of the river, you will go where you need to go.

The river of God's blessing is always flowing. Are you living in the main stream of His blessing, enjoying fellowship and closeness with Him, or are you stuck on the spiritual rocks of sin? Perhaps you've drifted complacently to water's edge, and now you're stuck.

The Bible says a sure way to enjoy God's blessing is to delight in His Word. We are blessed when we hide God's Word in our hearts, meditating on it day and night.

Do you want to enjoy the river of God's blessing? Then delight yourself in God's Word!

Father, I want to enjoy Your blessing today. Thank You for blessing me every time I read Your Word.

Week 24   Tuesday

ALWAYS AWAKE

He will not let your foot be moved; He who keeps you will not slumber. Behold, He who keeps Israel will neither slumber nor sleep. The Lord is your keeper; the Lord is your shade on your right hand.

Psalm 121:3-5

A frightened little girl came to her parents' bedroom. It was the third time she had come to their door that night. So her daddy got out of bed and walked her to her room, where he tucked her back in bed.

"Did you say your Bible verse?" he asked. She said, "Yes. I've said my Bible verse and my prayers. But I'm still scared."

The tired dad said, "Rachel, if something dangerous comes, I'm going to hear it because I'm the daddy. That's what I do. I listen for things so I can help keep you safe. You don't have to stay up and be afraid because I'm listening for you."

Knowing her daddy was always listening was all she needed to know. She slept the rest of the night.

Our heavenly Father is so much better than that tired daddy. He never sleeps. He is aware of everything at all times. When you are unsettled or afraid, remember the Lord is your keeper at all times. He hears and He sees, so you don't have to be afraid.

If you are afraid today, remember that the Lord of Heaven and earth is your keeper.

Father, when I am afraid, help me to trust in You.

Week 24   Wednesday

CHOOSE

And if it is evil in your eyes to serve the Lord, choose this day whom you will serve, whether the gods your fathers served in the region beyond the River, or the gods of the Amorites in whose land you dwell. But as for me and my house, we will serve the Lord.

Joshua 24:15

I once visited a street market in Central Asia where I noticed an unusual pair of athletic shoes for sale. On this one pair of shoes appeared the following marks: the Nike swoosh, the Adidas stripes, the Reebok vector, the New Balance "N," the silhouette of a Puma, and the K-Swiss shield.

What kind of shoes were they? They weren't any kind of shoes. They didn't stand for anything.

Many people say, "I believe in everything." If that is the case, then you really don't believe in anything at all.

Followers of Jesus Christ choose God's side. Trying to take both God's side and the world's side by standing in the middle is taking no side at all.

God is looking for people who will choose to stand firmly with Him even when it's risky. Spiritual heroes are men and women who determine that regardless of the personal cost, regardless of what friends and family and culture are doing, they will stand on God's side.

Whose side will you choose? Today, ask God to empower you by His Holy Spirit to firmly stand on His side and to be faithful to Him.

Father, today I choose to serve You. Help me to faithfully stand for You.

Week 24   Thursday

GOD HAS NOT MOVED

Jesus Christ is the same yesterday and today and forever.
Hebrews 13:8

An elderly couple driving in their truck passed a younger couple in a car. The young man's arm was around the young lady, whose head rested on his shoulder.

The older woman, seated on the passenger side of their truck, wistfully said to her husband, "Remember when we used to sit that close?" The old man smiled and said, "Honey, I haven't moved."

Do you remember a time when you were closer to God? Like the old man in the story, God has not moved.

God has not moved from His positions on holiness and purity. His positions on the sanctity of human life, on the sacredness of marriage, on sin and morality have not changed. God will never change His mind. Nor will He ever veer from His character.

When we deny the authority of God's Word and go our own way, we move further and further from Him. This is true for individual believers as well as for the church body.

God has not moved. Have you moved? If so, He invites you to move back to where He is. If you do, He will remove your feelings of isolation so you can enjoy His overwhelming presence.

Father, thank You so much that You do not change. If I have moved, please help me to come back to where You are.

Week 24

You Can Go Anywhere from Here

Therefore, if anyone is in Christ, he is a new creation. The old has passed away; behold, the new has come.
2 Corinthians 5:17

Two young men on a cross country trip stopped for gas at a small station, and sized up the area where they found themselves. It was nondescript and seemed unimpressive.

After filling their tank, they approached an old gentleman sitting outside the station. One of the young travelers said, "Excuse me, sir. Is there anything special about this little town?" The old man, who had lived there all his life, smiled and said, "Yes, sir, there is. The special thing about this place is, you can start from here, and go anywhere in the whole wide world."

Jesus, living His life through you, makes it possible for you to be what you could never become on your own. He can take you anywhere in the whole wide world in His name.

God gives us His strength in the midst of our weakness to bring Him glory. God specializes in making something out of nothing.

Do you fear you are not special enough for God to use you? Today, surrender yourself – all of who you are, including your weakness – to God. You will be amazed what He can do through a brand new creation.

Father, thank You for making me a new creation and empowering me to fulfill Your purpose for my life.

Week 25   Monday

GOD'S PATIENCE

The Lord is not slow to fulfill His promise as some count slowness, but is patient toward you, not wishing that any should perish, but that all should reach repentance.

2 Peter 3:9

An atheist said to one of his friends, "If there really is a God, then let him strike me dead." He waited for a moment, but nothing happened. "See, I just proved that there's no god." And his friend replied, "No, you just learned that God is very patient."

Are you running from God, resisting Him and His Son, Jesus Christ? God has been patient with you. He invites you this very moment to turn to Him.

God's patience will not last forever. There will come a time when God will stop being patient, and start pouring out judgment.

Today is the day to trust Jesus Christ. God does not promise to give you another opportunity to call on Him for salvation. The Bible always calls us to repent of our sin and turn to Jesus today.

You can call on Jesus Christ to save you right now. "Dear Lord Jesus, I am a sinner, and I ask for Your forgiveness. I believe You died for my sins and rose from the dead. I will follow You as my Lord and Savior. Please guide me and help me to do Your will."

This is a prayer God always answers.

Father, help me not run from You. Help me to obey You quickly when You call.

Week 25 — Tuesday

BEWARE OF THE SAFE PLACE

Therefore let anyone who thinks that he stands take heed lest he fall.

1 Corinthians 10:12

In 1911, a stunt performer named Bobby Leach became the first man to successfully go over Niagara Falls. He became an international sensation for his dare-devil stunt.

Then in 1926, while on a publicity tour in New Zealand, Bobby Leach slipped on an orange peel. He died two months later due to complications from the injury and the resulting infection. The man that had survived a trip over Niagara Falls was felled by piece of fruit.

Like most of us, Bobby Leach was not prepared for danger in what he assumed to be a safe situation.

We are wise to beware of the seemingly smooth path. Beware of the unguarded strength in your life. Beware of the temptation you think you've conquered and the sin you think you're immune to. Beware of that place where you think you are safe. Being too sure of ourselves can quickly lead to failure.

Satan has only to succeed once to wreak havoc in our lives, in our families, in a nation, or in a church. Never let your guard down because you feel you're in a safe place. We are only safe when we are faithfully following and obeying Jesus.

Father, help me to never ignore my weaknesses. Strengthen me every moment so I do not fall into sin.

Week 25   Wednesday

SUBMITTING TO AUTHORITIES

Let every person be subject to the governing authorities. For there is no authority except from God, and those that exist have been instituted by God. Therefore whoever resists the authorities resists what God has appointed, and those who resist will incur judgment.

Romans 13:1-2

Several years ago, I performed the funeral service for a friend who was in charge of the Transportation Security Administration at the Charlotte airport. Hundreds of TSA agents attended the service.

During the service, when I said, "Please stand," they all stood. When I said, "Please be seated," they sat. When I said, "Please bow your heads and close your eyes," they bowed their heads and closed their eyes. In that service, the TSA agents submitted to me.

But when I go through the security line at the airport, I submit to them. Whatever they tell me, I do it. At the airport, they have authority over me.

Unless it violates God's law, we are to obey our governing authorities. They are God's servants for our good.

Obey the law. Pay your taxes. Stop at red lights. Don't speed. If you do not obey, you will be punished by governing authorities, and rightly so. However, when we obey the law, we build a good reputation with those in authority, and we will have no reason to fear them.

More than anyone else, Christians should obey the law, and for no other reason than this: God commands it.

Father, help me to submit willingly to every authority You have placed in my life.

Week 25 — Thursday

HONOR THE EMPEROR

Honor everyone. Love the brotherhood. Fear God. Honor the emperor.
1 Peter 2:17

There is often a huge disparity between what we know to be right and the way our government rules. Christians in our current cultural climate are often at odds with the policies of government officials. So how can we keep the command to "honor the emperor?"

All government rule and authority is established by God. The Bible says, "Let every person be subject to the governing authorities. For there is no authority except from God, and those that exist have been instituted by God." (Romans 13:1)

The Holy Spirit moved Peter to write this command to honor the emperor while under the rule of a wicked government. Therefore, the command to honor those in authority is not only for those living under righteous governments. It is for everyone.

When you honor the authorities, you honor God who established them. By faith you can treat with respect and honor every official in authority over you, whether you agree with them or not. We can be obedient to them, unless the law violates God's commands. By doing this, you will be salt and light to the world, and will bring God glory.

Lord Jesus, help me to glorify You by giving honor and respect to those in authority over me.

Week 25

OBEYING GOD RATHER THAN MEN

And when they had brought them, they set them before the council. And the high priest questioned them, saying, "We strictly charged you not to teach in this Name, yet here you have filled Jerusalem with your teaching, and you intend to bring this Man's blood upon us." But Peter and the apostles answered, "We must obey God rather than men."
Acts 5:27-29

In Hitler's Germany, the Nazis pursued racist policies, and slaughtered millions of Jews. Pastor Martin Niemoller took a firm biblical stand in his pulpit, despite threats from the Nazis. As a result, he was thrown into a prison.

The prison chaplain was visiting prisoners when he came to Pastor Niemoller's cell. He asked Niemoller, "Why are you in prison?" Pastor Niemoller replied simply, "Brother, why are you not in prison?"

Most of the time, we can obey God and men. When you can obey God and men, do so. But when you cannot obey men and still obey God, then obey God, even when you face punishment.

The Bible clearly commands Christians to obey the law and to honor those in authority. However, when a government or anyone else in authority over us directs that we violate God's commands, then we must choose to obey God rather than men.

Remember, this world is not our home. Our citizenship is in Heaven, and Jesus Christ is our King. Entrust yourself to Him as you count the cost of obedience. He will strengthen you now, and reward your obedience to Him in the end.

Father, help me to always choose to obey You when the law of man conflicts with Your law.

Week 26 — Monday

A FAITHFUL FORTRESS

God is our refuge and strength, a very present help in trouble. Therefore we will not fear though the earth gives way, though the mountains be moved into the heart of the sea.

Psalm 46:1-2

A fortress is a structure built as a military stronghold. It is a place of protection from the enemy, and is strong without and within. Fortresses have been built from ancient times to protect people from the attacks of their enemies.

You can visit ancient fortresses around the world. In general, they are no longer used as hiding places. They are abandoned, and are good for nothing other than to teach history lessons. However, fortresses teach a valuable object lesson to followers of Jesus Christ.

The Bible speaks of God as a fortress and a refuge. The first line of the wonderful hymn, A Mighty Fortress is Our God calls God a mighty fortress, and a bulwark that never fails.

Almighty God is the fortress that never fails. His protection cannot be breached. His walls cannot be brought down. He is your hiding place, and your shelter from the enemy. He will never forget you; He will never forsake you. Today, trust in His unfailing protection.

Father, You are my strong protector. You never fail. Thank You that I am safe in You.

Week 26 — Tuesday

THE PRICE AND PRIVILEGE OF FREEDOM

For freedom Christ has set us free; stand firm therefore, and do not submit again to a yoke of slavery.

Galatians 5:1

Freedom is a lofty and wonderful aspiration. However, the cost of true freedom is steep. Freedom is never free. While Independence Day is a day of great celebration and fun for us, July 4, 1776, was a risky and life changing day for our courageous founding fathers.

Of the fifty-six signers of the Declaration of Independence, seventeen lost their fortunes, twelve had their homes destroyed, nine were killed in battle, five were arrested as traitors, and two lost sons in the Revolutionary War.

Just as signing that piece of parchment in Philadelphia's Independence Hall was a crucial moment for those men, determining to follow Christ is a defining event for the true believer.

Jesus said, "No one who puts his hand to the plow and looks back is fit for the kingdom of God." (Luke 9:62)

Following Jesus means laying down your will, your desires, your future, and even your life, if necessary, for His sake. True freedom is possible only by coming to Jesus on terms of complete surrender. True freedom is worth the cost.

Father, I have decided to follow You. Thank You for the high price You paid for my spiritual freedom!

Week 26   Wednesday

WHAT TO WEAR

Let us walk properly as in the daytime, not in orgies and drunkenness, not in sexual immorality and sensuality, not in quarreling and jealousy. But put on the Lord Jesus Christ, and make no provision for the flesh, to gratify its desires.

Romans 13:13-14

A little boy, learning about fire safety, was asked by the teacher, "Timmy, what should you do if your clothes are on fire?"

He smiled and immediately answered, "Don't put them on."

You can't argue with that logic. From a spiritual perspective, however, we often put on clothes that are already on fire. This happens when we purposely go places, adopt attitudes, and pursue relationships that are displeasing to God.

It is almost inevitable that we stumble into sin. However, it is inexcusable that we would run to sin. How can we make sure our garments are "flame retardant?" Here is the list of clothing to "put on" daily:

> The Armor of Light (Romans 13:12)
> The Lord Jesus Christ (Romans 13:14)
> The New Self (Ephesians 4:24, Colossians 3:10)
> The Full Armor of God (Ephesians 6:11, 13)
> Love (Colossians 3:14)
> Faith, Love and Hope (1 Thessalonians 5:8)

God has provided every believer a complete wardrobe that will help us obey Him and turn away from the desires of our flesh. Are you putting them on daily?

Father, help me to run from sin. I want to please You in my thoughts and actions today.

Week 26 — Thursday

STEALING FROM GOD

Will man rob God? Yet you are robbing Me. But you say, 'How have we robbed You?' In your tithes and contributions. You are cursed with a curse, for you are robbing Me, the whole nation of you. Bring the full tithe into the storehouse, that there may be food in My house. And thereby put Me to the test, says the Lord of hosts, if I will not open the windows of Heaven for you and pour down for you a blessing until there is no more need.

Malachi 3:8-10

Several years ago, a band of thieves robbed a string of churches on Sunday morning after the offerings had been received. As the monies were brought back for deposit, out came the bandits, who robbed the ushers of the entire offering.

The Bible says many people steal from God every week. They don't look like thieves. They come and go undetected, sitting in the pew, singing the songs, and listening to the sermon. Their crime? Holding back their tithes and offerings. They are robbing God.

The Bible says the tithe – the first ten percent of our income and increase – belongs to the Lord. So, if you are giving four percent of your income to the Lord, you are robbing Him of six percent. If you give eight percent, you are robbing Him of two.

Tithing is an opportunity to obey, trust, and show thanks to God. God issues a great promise: when you are faithful to give Him the full tithe, you won't have enough room to receive the blessings that God will pour out on you. God has promised to meet all our needs. Therefore, we can give generously and cheerfully!

Father, all I have is from You. I will give to You with a cheerful heart because of all You have given me.

Week 26   Friday

THE RIGHT FOUNDATION

According to the grace of God given to me, like a skilled master builder I laid a foundation, and someone else is building upon it. Let each one take care how he builds upon it. For no one can lay a foundation other than that which is laid, which is Jesus Christ.

1 Corinthians 3:10-11

Long ago, a church in Italy began construction of an impressive bell tower. Up, up, up rose the beautiful tower. However, it was not long before the builders, as well as passers-by noticed that the tower was not straight. By the time it was complete, the tower was about fourteen feet past perfectly vertical. Today, the faulty structure requires the regular interference of engineers to remain upright.

The famous landmark known as "The Leaning Tower of Pisa" leans because its foundation is inadequate to support its weight. The soil under the tower is comprised of clay, sand and shell – hardly sufficient to uphold such a weighty structure. The tower itself is beautiful and impressive, but on its own, it cannot stand. One day, it will fall.

There are many people whose lives are beautiful and impressive on the outside, but leaning on the inside. The foundation of your life is of primary importance. There is but one foundation that will hold you up to eternity, and that is Jesus Christ. Nothing else will ever be enough. Take care how you build your life, so that, in the end, it will stand.

Father, help me to build every aspect of my life upon the foundation of Jesus Christ and His Word.

Week 27   Monday

KEEP YOUR EYES ON THE PRIZE

Not that I have already obtained this or am already perfect, but I press on to make it my own, because Christ Jesus has made me His own. Brothers, I do not consider that I have made it my own. But one thing I do: forgetting what lies behind and straining forward to what lies ahead, I press on toward the goal for the prize of the upward call of God in Christ Jesus.

Philippians 3:12-14

In 1952, Florence Chadwick waded into the water off Catalina Island with the goal of swimming twenty-six miles to the California coast. An accomplished long-distance swimmer, she had been the first woman to swim the English Channel in both directions.

However, on this day, the fog was so thick that Florence could barely see the boats that accompanied her. After fifteen hours of determined swimming, Florence Chadwick abandoned her quest. Her crew of encouragers helped her into one of the boats.

Imagine her disappointment when she learned she had quit within just one mile of the end. Neither the cold nor exhaustion caused Florence's failure to endure. She gave up because she couldn't see the goal.

Many times we are tempted to give up spiritually because we simply lose sight of our goal. The fog of discouragement, hard circumstances, and past failures often prevent us from focusing on the goal of the upward call of God in Christ.

Today, keep your eyes on Jesus. He is the goal. Through His Word, He is always visible. Looking to Him will provide the encouragement you need to continue. There is a prize waiting for those who press on!

Lord Jesus, help me keep my eyes on You when I think I can't continue one more step.

Week 27   Tuesday

MUD PIES

Fear not, little flock, for it is your Father's good pleasure to give you the kingdom.

Luke 12:32

A little girl played in the mud at her grandmother's house. She was covered in brown soft mud from head to toe. The grubby little girl made three mud pies, decorated with pebbles and sticks, and placed them in the sun to bake. When her grandmother found her, she proudly showed her the pies. "When they're done, we can eat them!"

The grandmother said, "Honey, I've got five dollars. I'll buy those mud pies from you. I've got clean clothes for you, and I've made your favorite dessert. Why don't you come in, clean up, and we'll have lemon meringue pie."

When we acknowledge our great need and bring God the filthiness of our lives, He offers a great exchange. He gives us His eternal riches in exchange for our spiritual poverty. He gives His food in exchange for those things that will never nourish the soul. He gives His cleansing through the blood of His Son, Jesus Christ in exchange for our sin and unrighteousness.

God offers us His greatest wealth. It's His pleasure to do so! Confess to Him your spiritual poverty, and it will be His good pleasure to give you His kingdom and pour out His blessings on you.

Nothing I have on my own is worth keeping, Lord. Anything good I am or have on my own is filthy before You. Thank You for giving me all the riches of Your kingdom!

Week 27   Wednesday

BY MY SPIRIT

Then he said to me, "This is the word of the LORD to Zerubbabel: Not by might, nor by power, but by my Spirit, says the LORD of hosts."

Zechariah 4:6

I don't mind flying. It saves me a lot of time when I travel. But I don't like to fly through bad weather. Bouncing through the atmosphere at 35,000 feet is not my idea of a fun time.

I can peacefully endure the roughest flight by remembering one thing: I have no idea how to navigate through bumpy skies, but my pilot does. I have no skill to fly a plane, but he's an expert. It's my job to go, but it's his job to take me where I need to be. Remembering that helps me not be anxious.

Do you become fretful about your ability to do what God has asked of you? The Holy Spirit of God will strengthen and enable you to walk through whatever God asks of you. Through the Holy Spirit, you have all the power required to do what God wants you to do, to be who God wants you to be, and to accomplish what God has given you to accomplish.

Life will sometimes leave you feeling helplessly out of control. Don't depend on your own might or your own power. Instead, rely on God's Holy Spirit to do it through you.

Thank You, Lord Jesus, that You supply all the power I need to do all that You ask me to do by the power of Your Holy Spirit living in me.

Week 27   Thursday

WAR GAMES

For we do not wrestle against flesh and blood, but against the rulers, against the authorities, against the cosmic powers over this present darkness, against the spiritual forces of evil in the heavenly places.

Ephesians 6:12

People around the world are on heightened alert daily because for them, war is a way of life. Perhaps you are safe from missiles being lobbed over your head day and night. But there is a war going on that Christians are very much involved in, even if we can't see it. We call it "spiritual warfare."

Perhaps you fear spiritual warfare. Maybe you think the topic is only for the "super spiritual." You may even deny it exists. But spiritual warfare is real, and God has made complete provision for His children to be victoriously involved.

Satan would be perfectly happy for you to ignore the battle going on around you. However, going AWOL in spiritual warfare is not an option, unless becoming a spiritual prisoner of war is appealing to you.

As I've said before, God did not put you on a playground when He saved you. He put you on a battleground. However, He does not want you to grow weak in the knees at the thought of spiritual warfare. God has already won the war, so suit up, and don't be afraid of the battles.

Father, thank You for the armor You have provided to protect me in spiritual warfare.

Week 27

THE COYOTE'S AFTER YOU

Put on the whole armor of God, that you may be able to stand against the schemes of the devil.

Ephesians 6:11

As a kid, I loved Road Runner cartoons. Every Saturday, I watched Wile E. Coyote plot and carry out his silly schemes to catch the super-fast bird. Once in a while, the coyote's plan almost worked. But in the end, the coyote was always shamed in his ridiculous effort to catch his speedy prey.

Christians have an enemy who never stops scheming against us. Jesus said our adversary, Satan, has a simple, three-pronged plan: "To *steal* and *kill* and *destroy*." (John 10:10)

Satan wants to steal, kill and destroy your marriage, your kids, your witness, and the souls of precious people. Satan is enemy number one.

Because Satan has drawn a bullseye on our backs, we must daily put on every piece of the armor of God. Jesus has come that we might have life. His armor protects our life from the schemes of the enemy.

You can count on Satan coming at you with a plot to steal, kill, and destroy. But his schemes are no match for God's armor. God's armor has no vulnerable spots. When you wear it every day, you will be able to stand against everything the devil can throw at you.

Father, thank You that the armor You provide is sufficient to protect me from every weapon of the evil one.

Week 28 — Monday

THE ENEMY'S ARSENAL

...He was a murderer from the beginning, and does not stand in the truth, because there is no truth in him. When he lies, he speaks out of his own character, for he is a liar and the father of lies.

John 8:44

A successful military campaign is often most dependent upon a strong arsenal of weaponry. The weapons of physical battle are specific to the battle need. Spiritual warfare is the same. Our adversary, the devil, maintains an extensive and effective arsenal of weapons, ready to fire in your direction.

Perhaps his most harmful tactic against the Christian is a very subtle yet extremely effective weapon – deception. He first deployed this weapon in the Garden of Eden when he began a casual conversation with Eve. He only made one little suggestion: "Did God really say?" That day, Satan didn't raise a sword. He only had to raise a doubt. And with it, he took captive all of mankind.

There is only one counter-measure against deception: truth! The Bible says that the Word of God is truth and is our sword. It's the only offensive weapon God has given to complement the armor He provides every believer. So know what God's Word says and learn to handle it skillfully so you can identify the enemy's lies, especially the ones that sound very close to the truth. Be on your guard!

Father, help me to know Your Word well so I can recognize the enemy's deception.

Week 28 — Tuesday

WISDOM IN TRIALS

If any of you lacks wisdom, let him ask God, who gives generously to all without reproach, and it will be given him.
James 1:5

Henry Anhalt, his wife, and their three sons were flying aboard a small plane returning home to Florida from a mission trip when the pilot collapsed and died from a heart attack, leaving them with no one to bring them down.

Don McCullough, a flight instructor, responded to Henry's panicked calls of "Mayday!" He calmly talked Henry through the landing procedure, enabling Henry to successfully land the plane and deliver his family to safety.

Henry had not intended to learn to fly an airplane that day. He learned how because he was in a position that he *had* to learn how.

In the same way, trials teach us things that we would never learn otherwise. That is one reason we can "count it all joy" when we fall into all kinds of trials. Difficulties stretch us beyond our own strength, knowledge, and skills, so that we cry out to God, "Mayday! Mayday! Lord, I need your wisdom!"

God promises to give His wisdom liberally to all who ask. The moment we cry out to Him for wisdom in our trial, the Lord opens His hand and says, "Child, I'm so glad you asked. Here's all the wisdom you need."

Lord, today I need Your wisdom for _____. Thank You for giving me all the wisdom I need.

Week 28   Wednesday

TRIALS BRINGS VICTORY

Blessed is the man who remains steadfast under trial, for when he has stood the test he will receive the crown of life, which God has promised to those who love Him.

James 1:12

Trials come in all shapes and sizes. Some trials are brief, while some last our entire lives. Some impact us for a short time; some trials impact us for years. Regardless of the type of trial, they all have one thing in common – trials are trying! No trial is fun.

God says to be joyful when we encounter trials. You probably think, "Well, that's easier said than done!" For a person who doesn't know Jesus as Savior, rejoicing in trials might be impossible. However, it is entirely possible for the Christian.

God uses trials to bless us in ways we cannot experience when we walk smooth paths. Here are some reasons we can be joyful in trials.

Trials produce patience (James 1:3), develop maturity (James 1:4), increase our wisdom (James 1:5), strengthen our faith (James 1:6-8), and transform our perspective. (James 1:9-11) Trials transform us for our good.

And finally, God promises the "crown of life," a victor's crown, to all who remain steadfast when tested. When you trust God during a trial, you are automatically a winner! So, in whatever trial you are facing today, *count it all joy!*

Father, help me to be patient when I face trials, knowing You use them to make me more like Jesus.

Week 28 — Thursday

TRIALS BRING TEMPTATION

Blessed is the man who remains steadfast under trial, for when he has stood the test he will receive the crown of life, which God has promised to those who love him. Let no one say when he is tempted, "I am being tempted by God," for God cannot be tempted with evil, and He Himself tempts no one.

James 1:12-13

A pastor friend of mine awoke one Sunday morning to find the lower level of his home standing in almost three inches of water. To make matters worse, he learned the water had come from the outgoing rather than the incoming pipes. You can imagine the mess, the odor, and the frustration he experienced.

He might have responded in anger, yelling at his wife and kids, despairing over the difficulty of the clean-up, and becoming distracted so that he could not serve the Lord effectively that Sunday.

Instead, he trusted God. He surrendered his emotions to the control of the Holy Spirit, and determined to glorify God even while dealing with a very messy situation.

God uses trials to produce the best in us; but Satan shows up in our trials with the pressing temptation to act our worst. The mess in my friend's house presented a trial. The trial presented a temptation. But God redeemed the trial to strengthen his patience and prove his character.

We all face daily challenges of varying degree. Steadfastly trusting Christ in our trials creates a greater love for Him and qualifies us for the crown of life.

Father, when I am tempted by my circumstances, help me to be patient and respond to You in trust.

Week 28   Friday

THE LURE OF TEMPTATION

Let no one say when he is tempted, "I am being tempted by God," for God cannot be tempted with evil, and He himself tempts no one. But each person is tempted when he is lured and enticed by his own desire.

James 1:13-14

Michele and I once lived in a pretty little parsonage right next to a wheat field. After the harvest when the farmer mowed the field, the field mice packed their little bags and headed for the parsonage. Michele and I are nice people, but we do not share with mice.

We loaded several traps with bait and set them in the laundry room. The furry little intruders learned quickly that our home was not their cold-weather hotel.

The mice were lured to the traps because the bait appealed to them. But when the trap snapped shut, the mouse definitely regretted his decision.

God doesn't lure us to dangerous places. We are drawn to them by our own lusts for pleasure, power, freedom, recognition, riches, and acceptance – all things that appeal to our flesh.

Satan also sets his traps, baited with what we have an appetite for, and he can provide plenty of what our flesh wants.

Our desires may not be bad in themselves, but any of them has the potential to lure us into sin. Stay away from temptation! Stay in God's Word and in prayer, and steer clear of situations that can lead you to sin!

Lord, help me to stay away from things that I know are weaknesses for me.

Week 29   Monday

HOME ON THE RANGE

Or do you not know that the unrighteous will not inherit the kingdom of God? Do not be deceived: neither the sexually immoral, nor idolaters, nor adulterers, nor men who practice homosexuality, nor thieves, nor the greedy, nor drunkards, nor revilers, nor swindlers will inherit the kingdom of God. And such were some of you. But you were washed, you were sanctified, you were justified in the name of the Lord Jesus Christ and by the Spirit of our God.

1 Corinthians 6:9-11

"Oh, give me a home, where the buffalo roam, where the deer and the antelope play, where never is heard a discouraging word, and the skies are not cloudy all day."

Two buffalo had spent a great day roaming about their home on the range. The deer and the antelope played. There was not a cloud in the sky.

Later, a cowboy said to the buffalo, "You look disgusting! Your head's are too big, your eyes are too small, you've got bad breath, your hair is ugly, and you stink."

At that, one of the buffalo said, "I think we just heard a discouraging word."

We all want to hear encouraging words. But sometimes, an encouraging word is one that lovingly tells a hard truth. The truth is that we are sinners, our sin separates us from God, Hell is real, and we all deserve to go there. That can feel very discouraging.

But that's not the whole truth! God's own Son, Jesus Christ died to rescue us from Hell! He saves everyone who repents of sin and calls on His name. The gospel is the best encouraging word! Who can you encourage with the gospel today?

Father, make me ready today to share an encouraging word about Jesus with someone who needs to hear it.

Week 29   Tuesday

EXPERIENCE PRAYER

Rejoice always, pray continually, give thanks in all circumstances; for this is God's will for you in Christ Jesus.
1 Thessalonians 5:16-17

John's family owned an apple orchard, so John spent his entire life surrounded by apples. He knew about apples: how to develop the root systems, when to prune the trees, the best fertilizer to use, and when to pick them at their peak flavor.

John knew every variety of apples. He knew which apple worked best in which recipe. John knew everything about apples. But John never ate an apple.

One day as he walked through the orchards, for the very first time he reached up, pulled down a beautiful red apple, and ate it. Now, John really knew about apples. And it changed his life.

Do you want to know God's will? His will is for us to rejoice, pray, and give thanks. The Bible uses the words *"always," "continually,"* and *"in all circumstances"* to show when we should pray. Our days should be salted with prayer, always lifting thanks, rejoicing and requests to God.

Jesus taught about prayer. Bookstores are loaded with books about prayer. There are great sermons and Bible studies on prayer. Learning about prayer doesn't change your life or your circumstances, but praying does. Just pray.

Lord, help me to love to pray. Help me to pray every day, in every situation.

Week 29 — Wednesday

A Treasure Worth Finding

I appeal to you therefore, brothers, by the mercies of God, to present your bodies as a living sacrifice, holy and acceptable to God, which is your spiritual worship. Do not be conformed to this world, but be transformed by the renewal of your mind, that by testing you may discern what is the will of God, what is good and acceptable and perfect.

Romans 12:1-2

Suppose a man comes running up to you after church offering a $5000 reward to anyone who can find the valuable ring his wife has lost. Would you be eager to beat the church down the street to the restaurant for lunch, or would your focus be on finding the missing ring?

We would probably all look until the ring was found, because it was something so valuable.

God has something much more valuable for each of us to find – His will for us. It's the most precious thing you can know. God wants you to know His will, beginning with salvation through His Son, Jesus Christ.

God has never said to anyone who is earnestly seeking His will, "Sorry, I won't tell you." To find God's will, we tune our hearts to His voice through prayer and His Word, and live in obedience to what we already know of God's will.

The question is not so much how to know God's will for your life, but whether you are living in obedience to Christ, holy and surrendered to Him. When you are, He will reveal His good and perfect will for you in every situation.

Father, I desire to know Your will for my life. Help me to be obedient to You so I can discern Your will.

Week 29   Thursday

REMEMBERING YOUR PURPOSE

But whatever gain I had, I counted as loss for the sake of Christ. Indeed, I count everything as loss because of the surpassing worth of knowing Christ Jesus my Lord. For His sake I have suffered the loss of all things and count them as rubbish, in order that I may gain Christ.

Philippians 3:7-8

In 1629, when the favorite wife of Indian ruler Shah Jahan died, he ordered that a magnificent tomb be built as a memorial to her. The Shah placed his wife's casket in the middle of a parcel of land, and construction of the temple literally began around it.

Several years into the venture, however, the Shah's grief for his wife gave way to an overwhelming passion for the building project.

One day while he was surveying the site, he reportedly stumbled over a wooden box, and ordered workers to throw it out. Only months later did he realize that the discarded box was his wife's casket. The original purpose for the memorial tragically became lost in the details of construction.

Just as the ruler lost sight of his purpose, it's easy for us to forget our primary purpose. Paul said that he was willing to forsake everything else in his life in order to accomplish one simple, but eternally transformational, thing – knowing Jesus Christ.

The most important thing you can do every day is to keep your eyes fixed and your heart focused on knowing and pleasing Jesus Christ. Nothing is more important than knowing Him.

Lord Jesus, help me to set aside anything that keeps me from knowing You more today.

Week 29

Uncirculated or Spent?

But I do not account my life of any value nor as precious to myself, if only I may finish my course and the ministry that I received from the Lord Jesus, to testify to the gospel of the grace of God.

Acts 20:24

My wife has a United States proof set of coins from the year of her birth. The set contains five uncirculated coins: a fifty-cent piece, a quarter, a dime, a nickel, and a penny. Its value is ninety-one cents. Maybe you valuable coins in your home, kept in a safe place where they're protected, and you count them as precious to you.

Our lives are valuable. We do everything possible to shield ourselves and our families from anything that might cause any harm at all.

In many ways, that's commendable. However, if you are protecting yourself at the expense of obeying Jesus, that's a problem. God does not want us to treat our lives like a proof set of coins, valuable but never spent.

Christ-followers are called to pour ourselves into ministry and to spend ourselves for His glory, so that at the end of our lives, we, like Paul, can say, "I've done what Jesus Christ has called me to do. I have fulfilled my ministry."

Are you keeping your life safe and uncirculated, or are you spending it for the glory of God?

Lord Jesus, You are more valuable to me than anything on this earth. Help me to invest my life in Your kingdom.

Week 30   Monday

MULTIPLE CHOICE

Hear, O Israel: The Lord our God, the Lord is one.

Deuteronomy 6:4

I love multiple-choice tests. There is always at least a 25% chance of success just by guessing. However, even if there are multiple choices, each question has only one true answer.

For instance, two plus two equals four, not three, or five or seven. Even if you want another choice to be correct, and even if you don't understand why four is the answer, truth says two plus two equals four. I wouldn't walk across a bridge or fly in a plane built on incorrect math. It can be dangerous not to stick to the truth where math is concerned.

Truth in eternal matters is more important. The Bible says, "The Lord our God is one." That is narrow truth. Jesus said, "I am the way, the truth, the life. No one comes to the Father except through Me." (John 14:6) That is narrow truth. No other answer will hold up.

The narrow truth of the gospel is the glorious truth that saves everyone who trusts in it! It is the bridge from God to man that will never fail! Everyone who comes to the one true God, revealed through His one and only Son, Jesus Christ, will be saved.

Father, I believe that Your Word is truth. Help me to evaluate everything in my life according to Your Word.

Week 30 — Tuesday

TRAVELING COMPANIONS

Blessed is the one who does not walk in step with the wicked or stand in the way that sinners take or sit in the company of mockers, but whose delight is in the law of the Lord, and who meditates on His law day and night.

Psalm 1:1-2

A woman driving in a High Occupancy Vehicle lane – reserved for vehicles with two or more people – was pulled over by a patrolman. As he approached the car, his suspicion was confirmed. The woman's "passenger" was a stylishly dressed mannequin with a brunette wig and sunglasses.

The driver protested to the officer when he requested both her ID and that of her "passenger." "I don't see the problem with me driving around with a dummy in my car. Everyone else is doing it!"

She probably did not help her case with the officer by demeaning the intelligence of other drivers and their passengers. Whatever that lady may have meant about driving with a dummy, there's no question that God's Word warns us against traveling through life with foolish people.

Who are you listening to? Are you following the examples of the wise or the foolish? Who are you taking along with you for your ride through life? Listening to the so-called wisdom of fools will take you down the wrong path every time. Instead, strive to glean wisdom for your life from God's Word and those who obey it. God blesses those who love and obey His Word.

Father, I ask that You would transform me into the image of Christ as I behold Your glory day by day.

Week 30   Wednesday

TAKE THE BALL AND RUN

You shall love the Lord your God with all your heart and with all your soul and with all your might. And these words that I command you today shall be on your heart. You shall teach them diligently to your children, and shall talk of them when you sit in your house, and when you walk by the way, and when you lie down, and when you rise.

Deuteronomy 6:5-7

Paul "Bear" Bryant, the beloved football coach of the University of Alabama, told a story from his early days of coaching at the University of Kentucky.

Kentucky was playing Tennessee. Bear Bryant's Wildcats fumbled the ball right in front of the bench, and in the process, knocked over a whole box of footballs. Suddenly, there were nine footballs on the field. Coach Bryant shouted to his players on the field, "Pick 'em up! Pick up the balls!" Tennessee recovered five footballs, and Kentucky, four. The officials gave possession to Tennessee because they grabbed more balls than Kentucky.

Don't neglect to take the ball and run toward every opportunity to make disciples of Jesus Christ in your home. Faithfully teach your children and grandchildren to love God above all things. Open God's Word with them and read it together. Make discussion about spiritual things a regular part of your relationship with your family.

It is important to make a spiritual connection with your children and their children so you can help them know and love Jesus. God wants to use you to make an eternal impact in their lives. Raising children is your very best opportunity to make disciples.

Father, help me to take every opportunity to lead my children and grandchildren to Jesus.

148

Week 30   Thursday

OUR HIGHEST ASPIRATION

And we all, with unveiled face, beholding the glory of the Lord, are being transformed into the same image from one degree of glory to another. For this comes from the Lord who is the Spirit.

2 Corinthians 3:18

A dirty peasant girl came to the village square. She stood for some time before the beautiful statue of a noble and graceful woman. She gazed into the lovely face of the statue. Then, she went home and washed her face and combed her hair.

The next day, she returned, her face clean and her hair combed. Again, she studied the statue for a long time. She returned home, where she mended her tattered clothing so that it looked more like the dress she saw on the statue.

Daily, the girl visited the statue. Eventually her expression, her posture, her figure, and her face began to match that of the statue.

In the same way, Jesus Christ transforms us as we come to Him daily through His Word and through prayer. Meditating on Him gradually changes us into His image so that we can show Him to the world around us.

The Bible says that moment by moment, day by day, we are being transformed into the image of our glorious Lord Jesus. We behold His glory as we read His Word and pray. Being with Jesus sets us apart so the world can see Jesus in us.

Father, I ask that I behold Your glory; that You would transform me into the image of Christ.

Week 30

Truth or Consequences

A false witness will not go unpunished, and he who breathes out lies will not escape.

Proverbs 19:5

Sarah Adler, a noted stage actress of the early twentieth century, was never willing to admit her true age. One day, a nosy journalist asked, "Madame Adler, I don't mean to embarrass you, but would you tell me your age?" Without hesitation, she replied, "Sixty-eight."

The reporter objected, "But, how can that be? I just asked your son his age, and he told me he is sixty."

Sarah replied, "Well, he lives his life and I live mine."

Deception always comes back to haunt us. As those who have been transformed by Him who is "the way, the truth, and the life," believers in Christ are to be men and women of the truth.

Don't give in to the temptation to lie when you believe that lying would give you an advantage. Don't believe it's best to lie because it might save you embarrassment. Don't lie when you think it might be easier.

Pray for the Holy Spirit to guard your lips against untruthfulness today. And when you're tempted to lie, remember that the Spirit of truth dwells in you.

Father, help me to always tell the truth. Help me never to lie to make my circumstances better.

Week 31   Monday

WHAT IS SUCCESS?

...But whoever would be great among you must be your servant, and whoever would be first among you must be your slave, even as the Son of Man came not to be served but to serve, and to give His life as a ransom for many.

Matthew 20:26-28

How do you define success? Success means different things to different people.

For athletes, success may mean wins on the ball field, on the track, or in the gymnasium. Success may be measured by achievements, by wins, by attitude, by championships. For students, success might be defined by your classroom performance, your GPA, or whether you make the dean's list. In business, success can be defined by moves in your career, by your bottom line, or by your stock portfolio.

But, how does a follower of Jesus Christ define and achieve success? So many people don't really understand what Jesus has to say about success. His definition of success is radically different from the world's definition.

Jesus' kind of success says, "Serve. Don't look for people to serve you. Love God more than anything and love your neighbor as yourself. It's better to give than receive. Forgive as many times as you're offended. When you die to yourself, you'll live."

Following Jesus means radically redefining success. Jesus says that success is living a life of submission, service, and sacrifice, even when you're suffering.

Are you a success by Jesus' standard?

Father, help me to successfully follow You and serve other people.

Week 31   Tuesday

THE PERFECT PET

Why do you spend your money for that which is not bread, and your labor for that which does not satisfy? Listen diligently to Me, and eat what is good, and delight yourselves in rich food. Incline your ear, and come to Me; hear, that your soul may live; and I will make with you an everlasting covenant, My steadfast, sure love for David.

Isaiah 55:2-3

In the seventies, Pet Rocks were all the rage. They were billed as the perfect "no-work" pet. Gone were the headaches of feeding, grooming, walking, and bathing a real, furry pet. Pet rocks were no mess, no hassle. And they very quickly made their inventor a millionaire.

Isn't it crazy what people will spend money on? The Pet Rock fad may seem ridiculous today, but not when you consider that internet consumers have spent billions on items that don't even really exist, like virtual "candies" to help you win online games.

People have been willing to spend their money, their time, their affections, and their lives for empty things since the beginning of time. In Isaiah, God confronted His people about this very thing. On what do you spend your time and your money? Think about where you focus your energy and attention. What matters most to you? Does what you're living for have eternal value?

God alone can satisfy the deepest hungers of our hearts. Only when we incline our hearts to Him will we be filled with things that really satisfy. Loving Jesus with your whole heart will bring life and satisfaction to your soul.

Father, I confess that sometimes I value worthless things more than I value You. Help me to listen to You and receive good from Your hand so I can be satisfied.

Week 31   Wednesday

FORSAKING ALL FOR CHRIST

And going on from there He saw two other brothers, James the son of Zebedee and John his brother, in the boat with Zebedee their father, mending their nets, and He called them. Immediately they left the boat and their father and followed Him.

Matthew 4:21-22

In the movie *Indiana Jones and the Last Crusade*, Indiana Jones and his father finally find the prized Holy Grail in an ancient cave. However they are warned that the grail cannot be taken past the cave's seal or disaster will come. When the woman with them tries to take the relic past the seal, the ground opens under her and she falls into a bottomless chasm.

Then Indiana tries to retrieve the grail from the opening earth, holding onto his father with one hand while straining to reach the grail with the other. Then Indiana Jones's dad says to him, "Indiana, let it go." And he does because he cannot hold the hand of his father and continue to reach for the grail.

We can't hold onto Jesus with one hand and grasp for the temporal things of the world with the other. When Jesus calls us to follow Him, He also calls us to forsake the world. Whatever we reach for will be our master. It will hold our attention to the exclusion of anything else.

Have you forsaken everything for the sake of following Jesus? What do you need to let go of today to hold onto Christ?

Father, help me to let go of everything that tries to take my attention away from You.

Week 31   Thursday

VISION CHECK

Open my eyes, that I may behold wondrous things out of Your law.

Psalm 119:18

If you've ever been to an eye doctor, you've experienced the familiar ritual of being fitted for lenses. You sit in a darkened room, looking at an eye chart illuminated on a far wall. Then the doctor puts a series of lenses in front of your eyes and asks you a simple question over and over again: *Which one looks better?*

He asks this question over and over, while changing the strength of the test lenses until finally he has expertly determined exactly which lenses give you the best vision.

From a spiritual perspective, we all need corrected vision. The strength of our spiritual vision depends upon the lenses through which we look. If we take in our world through the lenses of secular thinking, satanic deception, selfish desire, popular opinion, or peer pressure, we'll wind up with a distorted view of life.

Looking at our world through the lens of God's perfect Word gives us perfect spiritual vision. It helps us see through God's eyes, which are always 20/20. If you want to see life clearly, avoiding pitfalls, and see what is good and perfect, then always look through God's Word.

Father, help me to view my world through Your Word.

154

Week 31

Faith, Feelings and Facts

But thanks be to God, who gives us the victory through our Lord Jesus Christ.

1 Corinthians 15:57

We all have the occasional restless night. Sleep eludes us, and the morning comes much too early. Then all of the sudden, it's six o'clock. The alarm sounds, and the clock shows a six and two zeros. Then comes the voice of an all-too-cheerful radio announcer. You look to the window and there is light. It's six o'clock, alright, but it sure doesn't feel like it.

We sometimes make the same mistake in our spiritual life, basing our confidence in Christ on how we feel rather than what God says in His Word. If you have been saved, no matter what your emotions may say, here's what God says about you:

> You are fully forgiven (Ephesians 1:7)
>
> You are alive to God and dead to sin (Romans 6:11)
>
> You are God's child (Galatians 4:4-6)
>
> God is working everything in your life together for good (Romans 8:28)
>
> You have a wonderful future and victory in Jesus Christ (1 Corinthians 15:57)

It's been said that emotions are a great servant, but a horrible master. Don't base your faith on how you feel. Instead, rest your faith on the truth of God's Word.

Father, thank You I can depend on Your Word to always tell me the truth, regardless of how I feel.

Week 32   Monday

YOUR SUPERNATURAL RESOURCES

Now to Him who is able to do far more abundantly than all that we ask or think, according to the power at work within us, to Him be glory in the church and in Christ Jesus throughout all generations, forever and ever. Amen.

Ephesians 3:20-21

Hattie Green lived in poverty, and closely guarded every penny. She ate cold oatmeal because it cost money to heat it. When her son's leg became infected, she spent such a long time searching for a doctor to treat him for free that the leg had to be amputated. She died arguing over the value of drinking skim milk.

After her death, it was discovered that Hattie Green's estate was valued at over a hundred million dollars. She had more money than all of the people she knew combined, but she chose to live as though her vast resources never existed.

Sadly, many Christians live spiritually poor lives. What a pity to ignore the great and wonderful riches available to us as believers in Jesus Christ. We are children of the King, and yet many times we choose to live like paupers.

Our heavenly Father has resources to meet your every need beyond all you can ask or think. What is it you need today? Do you need peace, hope, joy, rest, provision, wisdom, or strength? In Jesus Christ, all of the riches of God are yours. So give thanks and ask for what you need. God will supply!

Lord, I'm so grateful for Your riches available to me in Christ Jesus!

Week 32

Tuesday

RESOLVED

Look carefully then how you walk, not as unwise but as wise, making the best use of the time, because the days are evil.
Ephesians 5:15-16

The Bible says that if we're living by God's wisdom, we will make the best use of our time. We are accountable for every minute, hour, day and season.

Jonathan Edwards, the great preacher of the eighteenth century was spiritually wise beyond his years. When he was only nineteen years old, he wrote out seventy resolutions by which he lived his life. Here are only three of them:

> Resolved, never lose one moment of time, but improve it in the best profitable way I possibly can.

> Resolved, to live with all my might, while I do live.

> Resolved, that I will live so as I shall wish I had done when I come to die.

Jonathan Edwards resolved, in every moment, in every season, at every opportunity, that he was going to live his life for God's glory.

Living by that kind of wisdom results in a life that God blesses and uses. You don't have to be super spiritual to live by that kind of wisdom. Just make the decision today: "I'm going to live every moment that God gives, every day and every season of my life, seeking God's wisdom for God's glory."

Lord Jesus, help me not to waste Your gift of time today, but to use each moment wisely.

Week 32   Wednesday

MEASURING UP

...But as He who called you is holy, you also be holy in all your conduct, since it is written, "You shall be holy, for I am holy."
1 Peter 1:15-16

In elementary school, our math teachers told us regularly: "You need to learn the metric system. Soon, we'll be switching to it for all our measurements."

More than thirty years later, the metric system still has not yet caught on in America. We still weigh ourselves in pounds. We still measure distances in feet, yards, and miles. Only a few things have changed. We buy two liter soft drinks, but gallons of milk and gas.

How do you measure yourself? It is foolish to measure yourself according to someone else's standard. It's also foolish to set your own standard. The only acceptable standard is God's standard. His standard is perfection, which is impossible for us to meet on our own.

That's why Jesus Christ died on the cross for us. Through His sacrificial death and victorious resurrection, Jesus makes those who receive Him holy and completely acceptable in the eyes of God.

Can we measure up to God's standard on our own? Never. Can we measure up because we have trusted in Jesus? Absolutely!

Today, we can rejoice that the righteousness of Christ has been applied to our lives, bringing us the full acceptance of holy God.

Thank You, Father, that You fully accept me in Christ!

Week 32   Thursday

GOOD THINGS COME IN THREES

We give thanks to God always for all of you, constantly mentioning you in our prayers, remembering before our God and Father your work of faith and labor of love and steadfastness of hope in our Lord Jesus Christ.

1 Thessalonians 1:2-3

Just about everything in our universe exists in three parts. The physical universe exists as time, space, and matter. History is divided into past, present, and future. Space is measured in length, breadth, and height. Matter appears as solid, liquid, and gas. Why? Our universe bears the fingerprint of its Creator, our triune God: Father, Son, and Holy Spirit.

The Bible identifies our Savior as the *Lord Jesus Christ*. Each one of those three words specifically identifies God's Son. *Lord* identifies Jesus as our Master. We belong to Him. We follow and obey Him. He's the one in charge. He is our Lord.

Jesus identifies Him as our Mediator, the one who reconciles sinful man and holy God.

Christ identifies Him as our Messiah, God's anointed and chosen One who came to deliver us from sin and from death, from Satan and Hell.

The Lord Jesus Christ is our Master, Mediator, and Messiah. He provides His children three perfect resources for victorious living: faith, hope and love.

Our Redeemer is perfect! You can trust Him in every situation, because He is complete and all you need.

Lord Jesus, I praise You for being a perfect Savior!

Week 32 — Friday

CORRECTIVE DISCIPLINE

It is good for me that I was afflicted, that I might learn Your statutes.

Psalm 119:71

As kids, my friends Michael and Wesley were vacationing at the beach with their parents when they snuck off to the corner store and managed to buy two big cigars. They ducked around the corner, lit the cigars, and started puffing.

Then along came Michael's dad. He wasn't angry. Instead, he said, "Smoke 'em." The boys were relieved, thinking they'd gotten away with their foray into the adult world, at least until they became very sick, like first time smokers often do.

Michael's dad made sure the boys felt the effects of their cigar adventure. It worked. My friends immediately lost their taste for cigars.

God very wisely allows us to feel the sometimes agonizing consequences of our sin so we will repent of it and return to God in obedience. God's discipline is the result of His deep love for us. If He didn't love us, He would allow us to continue unchecked toward the destruction that sin brings.

Are you feeling the painful results of sin today? God mercifully invites you to repent of your sin today and return to Him. Jesus Christ paid for your sin, so you can experience God's mercy and forgiveness!

Father, thank You that Your discipline always comes from Your love for me. Help me to respond to Your discipline with true repentance.

Week 33   Monday

TRIVIAL PURSUIT

And He said to them, "Follow Me, and I will make you fishers of men."

Matthew 4:19

In the eighties, the game Trivial Pursuit was a cultural phenomenon. Now, almost everywhere you go – at restaurants, on airplanes, on your phone – you can access a trivia game to pass your time. The gameshow *Jeopardy* has even pitted man against computer to see who can spout out the most trivia the quickest.

We are tempted to pursue the trivial in our daily lives. But followers of Jesus Christ have a significant pursuit. Now, instead of chasing temporal things, God invites us to pursue His kingdom and His purpose. Our new pursuit is to glorify the Lord Jesus Christ with our lives and to fish for the souls of men.

We will glorify Jesus as we follow Him daily. When we follow Him in obedience, He makes us more like Him. When we are more like Him, we glorify Him. When we are more like Him, we will love what He loves – people.

Fishing for the souls of precious people by making the most of our relationships and investing our time and our resources to see people "caught" for the kingdom of God is a pursuit with eternal value.

Father, give me a heart to pursue the souls of precious people for Your kingdom. Help me love lost people like You do.

Week 33   Tuesday

BROKEN BIRD'S NESTS

The heart of man plans his way, but the Lord establishes his steps.

Proverbs 16:9

A farmer was going to burn a pile of brush. He saw a small bird's nest in the pile, so he destroyed the nest. A few days later, the farmer came back to discover the little bird rebuilding its nest. Time after time the farmer destroyed the nest, only to have the bird rebuild. After many attempts to rebuild, the bird finally gave up.

Can you imagine the bird's frustration? He surely thought the farmer was his enemy, when in reality the farmer was protecting the bird and its family from a place that was going to be burned to the ground.

We are prone to complain to God when He allows roadblocks on our journey. However, God sees infinitely further than we can see. He knows all that is beyond the furthest point we can see. The hindrances and trials we face in life are often acts of God's grace, protecting us from harm and preparing us for something better.

When your nest is torn apart, remember that God is directing your steps. He's working in every circumstance of your life to bring about His glory and to work for your good.

Father, help me to trust You when my plans are interrupted.

Week 33 — Wednesday

DEAD ZONES

For I am sure that neither death nor life, nor angels nor rulers, nor things present nor things to come, nor powers, nor height nor depth, nor anything else in all creation, will be able to separate us from the love of God in Christ Jesus our Lord.
Romans 8:38-39

What did we ever do without cell phones? I love that I can always be connected to my family with a cell phone. However, there is one little inconvenience with using them: dead zones. In remote areas there may be little or no cell service available, resulting in dropped calls, or phone conversations that sound like they're from outer space. Dead zones adversely affect communication.

God's Word assures us that when we are in Christ, we never need to worry about a dead zone in our connection with God. In Christ, we are always in the "life zone." God always hears, always answers, and always loves and cares for us. Praise the Lord there are no dead zones with Jesus!

Nothing can separate you from the love of God in Christ Jesus. Death can't separate you from God's love. Your circumstances can't separate you from God's love. Neither your past nor your future can separate you from God's love. No earthly or heavenly authority can separate you from God's love. No lofty idea can separate you from God's love. No deep trouble can separate you from God's love. Nothing in the entire universe can separate you from God's love!

Father, I thank You today for Your love for me that never, ever fails!

Week 33   Thursday

GET IT RIGHT AT THE TOP

Behold, I will send you Elijah the prophet before the great and awesome day of the LORD comes. And he will turn the hearts of the fathers to their children and the hearts of children to their fathers, lest I come and strike the land with a decree of utter destruction.

Malachi 4:5-6

I always button my dress shirts from the top down. If there's an extra hole or an extra button when I get to the bottom, I know I didn't get the top button in the right hole. My shirt won't be right unless I unbutton every button and start all over. My mistake will not only be noticeable to me, but everyone will see that I didn't properly line up the buttons from the top down.

Dads, God has assigned you as the spiritual leader of your home. To be successful as a husband and a dad, your relationships must be right from the top down. The top "button" is your relationship with God. It won't matter how well everything else is buttoned up. Relationships with your wife and your kids just won't line up correctly when your relationship with God is not right.

Is your heart right with God today? Have you come to Jesus Christ and trusted Him for your salvation? Are you following Him as the Lord, the ruler of your life? Are you exhibiting the character of God the Father in your relationship with your children? Make sure everything is buttoned right at the top.

Father, help me to be right with You today so I can be right with my family and all the other relationships in my life.

Week 33

Friday

LABOR NEGOTIATIONS

Peace I leave with you; My peace I give to you. Not as the world gives do I give to you. Let not your hearts be troubled, neither let them be afraid.

John 14:27

A young woman was interviewing for a new job, and it looked like she would get it. So, she began to ask some questions of her own.

"At my last job, the company paid for all of my insurance. They gave me a Christmas bonus, a month of vacation, two hour lunch breaks, and free childcare. I also had unlimited sick leave. Can you give me all that?"

"We'll have to talk about those things," said her interviewer. "Why would you leave a company that gave you all that?"

"The company went bankrupt!" she replied.

There are no perfect situations in this life. No perfect families, no perfect churches, no perfect job. Every set of circumstances has its troubles. However, we can experience real joy and peace in every imperfect situation when we are trusting in Jesus Christ.

Jesus promised that, while we are in this world, we will have tribulation. But He follows it up with a tremendous encouragement: "But take heart; I have overcome the world." (John 16:33)

What tribulation are you facing today? You can rejoice that Jesus Christ gives rest to those who labor and peace for those who are troubled.

Father, thank You that I can enjoy Your peace in the midst of trouble. Help me not be anxious or afraid.

Week 34   Monday

GONE, GONE, GONE

"For which is easier, to say, 'Your sins are forgiven,' or to say, 'Rise and walk?' But that you may know that the Son of Man has authority on earth to forgive sins"—He then said to the paralytic—"Rise, pick up your bed and go home." And he rose and went home.

Matthew 9:5-7

I like to use a calculator when balancing my checkbook. My favorite button on my calculator is the "CE" button. If I enter a wrong number, I just press "CE", and it clears my error. There's no limit to the number of times I can clear the calculator of my mistakes.

When I was a little boy, we sang the following song in Sunday school: "Gone, gone, gone, gone! Yes, my sins are gone. Buried in the deepest sea; yes, that's good enough for me; I will live eternally. Praise God, they're G-O-N-E, gone." When God forgives our sin, they're gone, just like the cleared mistakes in my calculator.

There is no sin that cannot be covered by the blood of Jesus Christ. We can be certain that Christ's death covers every sin because God raised Jesus from the dead. If there was a sin that Jesus's death could not cover, then He would still be in the grave.

If you are trusting Jesus Christ for your salvation, you can have confidence that all your sins are forgiven and "gone, gone, gone" from God's ledger.

Father, thank You for cleansing me from every sin by the blood of Jesus Christ!

Week 34 — Tuesday

ARE YOU SAVED?

And it shall come to pass that everyone who calls upon the name of the Lord shall be saved.

Acts 2:21

For every person, life's greatest questions are, "*Where did I come from?*" and "*Where am I going?*"

There is only one answer to the first question. The Bible says God made us in His image. We are His creation. However there are two possible answers to the question, "*Where am I going?*" Are you going to Heaven or are you going to Hell? In other words, *are you saved?*

You might respond, "I've always been saved. My parents are Christians. I go to church every Sunday. I've been baptized. So I'm going to Heaven." But none of these things will take you to Heaven because none of them will save you.

The gospel has the power to save every person who calls on the name of the Lord Jesus Christ. The gospel is simply this: God's Son, Jesus Christ died on the cross to pay the penalty for our sin. He was buried and rose from the grave on the third day. Every person who places their faith in Jesus Christ will be saved.

Are you going to Heaven or to Hell? Nothing is as important as answering this question. If you are not saved, this very moment you can turn from your sin and trust Jesus Christ to save you. Then you can answer confidently, "I am going to Heaven!"

Father, thank You for saving me! Thank You for the promise of spending eternity with You in Heaven.

Week 34   Wednesday

A FUTURE RESOURCE

We give thanks to God always for you all, making mention of you in our prayers, remembering without ceasing your work of faith, labor of love, and patience of hope in our Lord Jesus Christ in the sight of our God and Father.

1 Thessalonians 1:2-3

Financial wisdom says we should be putting aside money for our senior years. If you are young, that may seem a long way off. But, as we age, knowing that a retirement account awaits us to meet our later needs provides a level of comfort in our present circumstances.

Financial resources we set aside for the future can evaporate like our next breath. But there is a certain future awaiting every follower of Jesus Christ. Knowing that Jesus will return and that we will live with Him forever helps us bear up under hard circumstances now.

So when the doctor says "It's cancer," or the boss says "Your services are no longer needed," when your spouse says he's leaving, when war and crime cause you to fear, or when life is just hard, you can endure with patience because your hope is in Jesus.

Our hope in Christ is not the world's wishful thinking. Our hope is based on God's unfailing promise that Jesus will return. We can patiently stand up under whatever the world throws at us, because Jesus is coming back!

Jesus I look forward to Your return! Help me to keep that in mind in the difficult moments of my life.

Week 34 — Thursday

THE RISK OF FORGIVING

And no longer shall each one teach his neighbor and each his brother, saying, "Know the Lord," for they shall all know Me, from the least of them to the greatest, declares the Lord. For I will forgive their iniquity, and I will remember their sin no more.

Jeremiah 31:34

Two sisters had carried on thirty-year feud. When one sister learned the other was ill, she felt compelled to visit. From her sickbed, the offended sister said in a faint voice, "The doctors say I'm seriously ill, Alice. If I die, I want you to know you're forgiven. But if I pull through, things stay as they are!"

So many people make the foolish choice to hang on to bitterness or anger rather than truly forgiving. What does it mean to forgive?

God's forgiveness is multi-layered. It pardons our sins and relieves us of sin's debt. It lifts the weight of guilt from our shoulders. And it sets us free to love and serve God without the cloud of sin hanging over us. When God forgives, He also forgets.

We cannot earn God's forgiveness. It is a wonderful gift that we simply receive from Him. Then, as we have been forgiven by God, we are to be like Him in extending that same forgiveness to others who have sinned against us.

Today, thank God for His complete forgiveness. Then ask Him to enable you to extend His kind of forgiveness to others.

Father, thank You for Your forgiveness and for freeing me from the guilt of my sin. Help me truly forgive everyone who offends me.

Week 34 — Friday

"MUTANT" CHRISTIANS

Evidently some people are throwing you into confusion and are trying to pervert the gospel of Christ. But even if we or an angel from Heaven should preach a gospel other than the one we preached to you, let them be under God's curse!

Galatians 1:7-8

Peter Parker was a normal young man until the day he was bitten by a radioactive spider and became Spider Man. Overexposure to gamma radiation turned mild-mannered scientist Bruce Banner into the Incredible Hulk. In comic books, radioactivity causes mutations that change normal people into characters they were never meant to be.

Many people follow a mutated gospel and a Christian faith that is totally different from biblical Christianity. This is happening more and more in our culture as people embrace less and less of biblical truth and expose themselves to false teachers. It is especially virulent in the younger generation.

We must hold fast to the Scriptures, teaching the infallible Word of God to the next generation and sharing the saving gospel of Jesus Christ without backing down. We must join the fellowship of believers in a Bible teaching church, setting an example that will give our children an anchor that will hold them throughout their lives. It will give our families a firm foundation and a place of refuge.

Let's be determined to live radically for Jesus, keeping our eyes on things above. That will give our kids something solid to hold to.

Father, help me to cling to the pure gospel of Jesus Christ and Your perfect Word.

Week 35   *Monday*

WORK IT OUT!

Therefore, my beloved, as you have always obeyed, not as in my presence only, but now much more in my absence, work out your own salvation with fear and trembling, for it is God who works in you to will and to act in order to fulfill His good purpose.

Philippians 2:12-13

Caterpillars come in all colors, shapes, and sizes. But they all pull themselves across the stems and leaves of plants, chewing their way through life. There's nothing graceful about caterpillars. They just crawl and chew.

Finally, they cocoon themselves away, tucked away, hidden in secret until the big reveal. When the cocoon finally splits open, out comes a beautiful butterfly.

What if, instead of fluttering about on the breeze and sipping nectar from colorful flowers, the butterfly crawled from plant to plant, chewing leaves as before? Wouldn't it be sad for him to ignore the reality of his wonderful new life and continue to live the old?

Christians are commanded to "work out your own salvation with fear and trembling." That simply means this: if you're a butterfly, don't live like a caterpillar! Real faith in Jesus changes who we are and what we do. It empowers us to turn from dark and hurtful things to what is right, true, and spiritually healthy. It transforms the way we think, talk, and treat other people.

If you are saved, your new life will work its way out into your actions and thoughts. Don't waste your new life. Work it out!

Father, help my life to provide evidence of the transformation You have done in me through Christ.

Week 35   Tuesday

HAVE YOU CAUGHT ANYTHING?

Passing alongside the Sea of Galilee, He saw Simon and Andrew the brother of Simon casting a net into the sea, for they were fishermen. And Jesus said to them, "Follow Me, and I will make you become fishers of men." And immediately they left their nets and followed Him. And going on a little farther, He saw James the son of Zebedee and John his brother, who were in their boat mending the nets. And immediately He called them, and they left their father Zebedee in the boat with the hired servants and followed Him.

Mark 1:16-20

Patience, skill, discernment, and persistence are necessary to be a successful fisherman. But even the best fisherman experiences disappointment when, at the end of the day, the stringer is as empty as the boat's gas tank.

After Jesus was raised from the dead, He went to find His disciples. They were in their boats after a disappointing night of fishing. Their nets were empty. These were the very same men Jesus called in the beginning of His ministry and promised to make "fishers of men." The scene was just like a repeat episode of your favorite television show.

Jesus instructed them to cast their nets again, this time on the other side of the boat. They obeyed, and so many fish filled their nets that they were unable to pull them all back to the shore. On their own, the disciples had done everything that effective and trained fisherman would do. But Jesus was responsible for filling the net with fish.

Don't mistake being an obedient fisherman with bearing the responsibility for the number of fish you catch. That's the Holy Spirit's job. We are to be faithful fishermen, and leave the results to Jesus!

Father, as I share the gospel in obedience to Your command, help me to patiently wait for people to accept You as Savior and Lord.

Week 35   Wednesday

CHERISH EACH OTHER

However, let each one of you love his wife as himself, and let the wife see that she respects her husband.

Ephesians 5:33

Marriages change over time. The overwhelming tenderness and concern husbands and wives feel for one another at the beginning of their marriages can, over the years, turn into defensiveness and criticism.

God's plan for marriage, however, is that we would continually cherish and nurture our spouses.

By God's design we each have a need for security, for self-worth, and for significance. At the deepest level, these needs can only be met by a growing relationship with Jesus Christ. But God established Christian marriage to give us an intimate and permanent relationship with another person who can help meet those deep needs in our lives.

Husbands, are your actions to your wife loving? Do you nourish and cherish her as you do your own body? Wives, does the way you speak and act toward your husband communicate respect and admiration for him?

As you serve each other and serve the Lord together, your marriage can make a positive contribution, not only to your earthly family, but also to God's kingdom as a whole. Marriage is ultimately a picture of Christ and His bride, the Church. Let's do well in our marriages in order to glorify Jesus Christ to the world.

Father, help me to truly cherish my spouse today. Help my love for my spouse to remain warm and not grow cold.

Week 35   Thursday

IT'S THE LAW

If Your law had not been my delight, I would have perished in my affliction. I will never forget Your precepts, for by them You have given me life.

PSALM 119:92-93

We've heard it said that gravity is not just a good idea; it's the law! Even if we voted to repeal the law of gravity, you would still fall to the ground if you jumped from your roof. Man-made laws can be changed, but it's impossible to alter God's laws.

In addition to the physical laws of nature, God has established the moral law in the Ten Commandments, and the spiritual laws that accompany them. The spiritual law says that sin – breaking God's law – leads to death and separation from God. The shedding of blood is required for sin to be forgiven. The spiritual law also says that when the acceptable sacrifice is made, God extends His forgiveness and gives us life.

God, in His great love, has provided the only acceptable sacrifice for sin in the death of His own Son, Jesus Christ! We cannot change God's law, but it can change us! Receiving God's forgiveness through Christ changes us from the inside out. Then, as we seek to obey God's commands, even in the small details of our lives, we begin to experience greater joy, greater peace, and greater freedom.

Father, I thank You that Your law is for my good. Forgive me when I break Your law and help me to experience Your joy when I obey.

Week 35

Friday

HANG IN THERE!

I have learned in whatever situation I am to be content. I know how to be brought low, and I know how to abound. In any and every circumstance, I have learned the secret of facing plenty and hunger, abundance and need. I can do all things through Him who strengthens me.

Philippians 4:11-13

A teenage boy was told by his father to dig up a large plant and move it to the back yard. The dad watched from the window as his son dug around the plant. When he reached the root, the boy was unable to get his shovel under the plant to pry it from the hole. He tried pushing it over, pulling it up, and dragging it out, all with no success. It was just too big.

His dad came to the frustrated boy and said, "Son, you haven't used all the power available to you."

"It's too hard, Dad! I can't do it!" the boy complained. The father said, "You haven't used all the power available to you. You didn't ask for my help."

God promises His abundant strength to help you do anything He asks of you. He has all the grace, all the power, all the comfort, and all the tools necessary for every task He assigns you. Don't fail to ask God to help you. He will gladly give you all the strength you need. Your job will often be too hard for you, but it is not too hard for you with God's help.

Father, today _____ feels too hard. I can't do it without Your strength. Please help me!

Week 36   Monday

STRAINING AT THE LEASH

I know, O Lord, that the way of man is not in himself, that it is not in man who walks to direct his steps.

Jeremiah 10:23

Our little Yorkshire terrier, Joey, weighs less than five pounds. When we walk Joey, his tiny legs require perhaps thousands of steps to keep up with us, but he makes the walk with gusto. It's the highlight of his doggie day!

Joey is easily distracted by other dogs, or by interesting smells and sounds. His eyes light up and his legs begin to spin like whirligigs as he starts after whatever has captured his attention.

That's why we walk Joey with a leash. It makes us able to correct him when he gets sidetracked and put him back on the path.

In a similar way, while we may make our plans, it is the Lord who orders our steps. He determines how our plans will work out, and only those plans that He has approved for our lives will ultimately succeed. We should be thankful that the Lord always holds the leash of our lives in His sovereign hands, protecting us from foolish choices and diversions as we follow Him.

Today, don't strain at the directing hand of God on your life. Trust Him, listen to Him, and obey Him. His paths are always the best.

Lord, I've made many plans. Would You please interrupt the plans in my life that are not according to Your plan for me?

Week 36   Tuesday

RUMBLINGS

Therefore, stay awake, for you do not know on what day your Lord is coming.

Matthew 24:42

In 79 B.C., the explosion of Mount Vesuvius wiped out the Roman cities of Pompeii and Herculaneum. The destruction was swift and devastating. Men and women were at the market. The rich were in their luxurious baths. In the middle of a very routine day, every life was suddenly snuffed out by tons of ash and lava. Even family pets suffered the same quick and final fate.

But was the eruption of Vesuvius really so unexpected?

Scientists have confirmed that weeks of rumbling and shaking, as well as an ominous plume of smoke coming from the top of Vesuvius, foreshadowed the devastating volcanic eruption. If the people had taken the warning signs more seriously, they might have escaped with their lives.

The Bible says there are "rumblings" in our world that point to the return of Jesus Christ. War, earthquakes, economic meltdown, increased lawlessness, and broken families all point to a coming day of judgment. When we hear those rumblings, it should move us as believers to live holy lives, and to share the gospel more passionately and pray for those around us who do not know Christ.

Jesus is coming soon. Keep watching. Keep praying. Keep sharing the gospel.

Father, help me to be watchful, living every moment to please You as I wait for Your return.

Week 36 Wednesday

BE A DISCIPLE, MAKE DISCIPLES

And He said to them, "Go into all the world and proclaim the gospel to the whole creation."

Mark 16:15

Michele and I have a great dog that lives by this motto: love all people, hate all dogs. Joey barks and goes crazy any time he sees another dog. So we spent twenty dollars for a little box that emits a high pitched sound that's irritating to dogs every time Joey barks. It's supposed to break Joey from barking.

Here's what we spent twenty dollars to discover: Our dog's commitment to barking is greater than any irritation this thing can create.

As followers of Jesus Christ, our motto should be: Be a disciple, make disciples. Are you as committed to sharing the gospel as my dog Joey is to barking? Nothing stops Joey from barking. What stops you from sharing the gospel?

Jesus final command to us to share the gospel to the whole creation should be our daily mission. Every morning, before our feet hit the floor, we should ask the Holy Spirit to give us opportunities to share a good word about Jesus with someone who needs to hear it. We should go about our days with open eyes and ears, looking and listening for every opportunity to tell someone about the saving grace of Jesus Christ. Nothing should stop us from sharing the greatest message on earth.

Father, I don't share the gospel as faithfully as I should. Forgive me, and give me a renewed passion to tell people about Jesus.

Week 36 — Thursday

SIN SHOCKED

"If you do well, will you not be accepted? And if you do not do well, sin is crouching at the door. Its desire is for you, but you must rule over it."

Genesis 4:7

We all know that an electric shock from your stove can kill you. But your electric clock is pretty small. It couldn't cause much harm if you touch its wires. Or could it?

A naïve repairman may not have sufficient respect for the lethal power of electricity. "A small shock might hurt a little," he tells himself, "but I can always just let go of the wire."

What the amateur doesn't realize is that even a small amount of electricity has the power to paralyze the muscles in your body – including your heart – making it all but impossible to let go. That's what makes it so dangerous.

Sin works the same way. People treat sin lightly because they don't fear its power to paralyze their souls. Too many people have foolishly grabbed hold of a sin that they later find they can't let go of, even when it's hurting them.

Sin is dangerous in our lives because it sets in motion destructive forces that we are powerless to stop.

Next time you're tempted to dabble in some seemingly small sin, remember this: God's warnings against sin in His Word are meant for your protection. Sin is never safe.

Father, help me to not justify committing "little" sins.

Week 36   Friday

WHAT'S YOUR PURPOSE?

Keep your conduct among the Gentiles honorable, so that when they speak against you as evildoers, they may see your good deeds and glorify God on the day of visitation.

1 Peter 2:12

A teacher noticed one of her more timid students was having trouble doing her math assignment. The teacher went to her quietly and asked if she needed help, knowing she probably wouldn't raise her hand.

When the problem was sorted out the little girl thanked the teacher, who told her not to be shy about asking questions. "That's one of the reasons I am here."

The little girl thought about that for a moment and asked, "What's the other reason?"

Do you know the reason you're here? Do you know your purpose?

Your purpose and my purpose is to glorify God so that when people look at our lives, they see the greatness of God working through us. That's why God created us. That's why Christ redeemed us.

God is glorified through us in many ways. When we give thanks, live holy and pure lives, give sacrificially, and have patience in suffering, God is glorified.

God is also glorified when sinners repent and trust in Christ for salvation. Therefore, God is glorified when we share the gospel. Does your life reflect this purpose? Does your life bring glory to Jesus Christ?

Father, thank You for giving my life meaning and purpose. Help me to glorify You in all I do.

180

Week 37   Monday

THE AMBITION BOMB

Do nothing from selfish ambition or conceit, but in humility count others more significant than yourselves. Let each of you look not only to his own interests, but also to the interests of others.

Philippians 2:3-4

A Virginia state trooper became a local celebrity almost overnight when it was reported that he had located bombs in two shopping malls, a courthouse, and a sports arena. However, his notoriety took a dramatic turn when officials learned that he had actually planted the explosives in an attempt to bolster his image. This man had a bad case of selfish ambition.

There's great value in having an ambition to please the Lord and accomplish His work. But our sinful nature can easily turn that ambition inward, causing us to try to gain an advantage over others or to attempt to garner recognition for ourselves, regardless of the cost. The results of such selfishness are usually explosive.

Putting the needs and desires of others before our own will help us to steer clear of selfish ambition. When Jesus died on the cross, He placed our need for salvation before His own desire to avoid pain. If He had placed His needs above ours, we would still be lost.

Godly humility is the remedy for selfish ambition. When we have the same attitude that Jesus had, our relationships and our lives will be changed.

Father, help me to be like You and to consider others more important than myself.

Week 37 Tuesday

SOMEONE WHO UNDERSTANDS

And the Word became flesh and dwelt among us, and we have seen His glory, glory as of the only Son from the Father, full of grace and truth.

John 1:14

Years ago, work crews marked construction sites by putting out smudge pots, oil burning devices with open flames.

One day, a four-year-old girl named Sarah got too close to a smudge pot, catching her pants on fire. The scars that resulted from her burns looked like a jigsaw puzzle running the length and breadth of her legs.

Several years later, Sarah was asked, "If you could have one wish, what would it be?"

Sarah wrote: "I want everyone to have legs like mine."

Perhaps you have felt the same way that Sarah did. When we suffer, we want other people to understand. We want others to be able to identify with us.

Jesus Christ, God in the flesh, identifies with all of our pain. He suffered not only the physical pain of a violent death on the cross, but the emotional pain of rejection and the spiritual pain of separation from God the Father.

Whatever your pain or weakness is, Jesus Christ knows exactly what you are going through. And because He can identify, He is able to strengthen, comfort, and encourage you in every way.

Lord Jesus, I'm thankful that You completely understand my weakness. I need Your strength and encouragement today!

Week 37   Wednesday

SKI MASKS, MACHINE GUNS AND THE PEACE OF GOD

"What are you doing, weeping and breaking my heart? For I am ready not only to be imprisoned but even to die in Jerusalem for the name of the Lord Jesus."

ACTS 21:13

In 2000, James was on his first mission trip to Kosovo, a volatile war-torn region in Europe. After a day of delivering aid to refugees, his team was stopped on their drive home from an evening worship service by six soldiers wearing ski masks and carrying machine guns. All but the driver were ordered from the vehicle.

Imagine James's fear at coming face to face with a group of rebels. As James prayed, he experienced tremendous peace. In a few moments, the passengers were allowed back into the van to continue their journey. It turned out that the men at the roadblock were part of a peace-keeping force. The ski masks were simply for warmth.

James learned in those crucial moments that he was ready to die for his faith. Like the apostle Paul, he knew the dangers that awaited him. But, to him, the souls of those who needed to hear the message of Jesus far outweighed his own safety.

There is no price too dear, no distance too far, no sacrifice too painful, no risk too great, and no cost too high to take the gospel to the ends of the earth.

Lord, help me be willing to take the gospel to everyone without being afraid, trusting You to take care of me.

Week 37   Thursday

CHANGE IS ALREADY HERE

When they came to Jesus, they saw the man who had been possessed by the legion of demons, sitting there, dressed and in his right mind; and they were afraid.

Mark 5:15

Almost every man in America who finds the right girl offers her a diamond ring when he proposes marriage. How do you think your girl would respond if you pulled open a velvet box, revealing a ring carefully set with a good sized lump of coal? Chances of her saying "yes" go way up if you replace the coal with a diamond.

Every diamond was once a dusty black lump of coal. It's a great picture of the transformation Jesus Christ works in us when we are saved. Don't be discouraged if you don't see immediate dramatic changes when you are saved. Instead, think about the ways we are instantaneously transformed at the moment of salvation:

> We go from being dead in our sin to being made alive with Christ.
>
> We go from being condemned by God to being forgiven by Him.
>
> We go from being an enemy of God to being reconciled to Him.
>
> We go from being slaves to sin to being free in Christ.

As you grow in your relationship with Jesus and obey God's Word, you'll experience more and more transformation. Old things have passed away and the new has come!

Father, I praise You for already transforming my life in wonderful ways, and that You won't stop changing me until I am in Heaven with You.

Week 37

Friday

GOD ANSWERS PRAYER

But as for me, my prayer is to You, O Lord. At an acceptable time, O God, in the abundance of Your steadfast love answer me in Your saving faithfulness.

Psalm 69:13

A man fishing on the coast in Atlantic City spotted a plastic bag floating in the water. Inside the bag were about 300 letters containing anguished prayer requests – most unopened – that had been mailed to a local pastor who had died two years earlier. Relatives had probably dumped the letters as garbage after his house was cleaned out.

Every letter was from a person crying out to God. Some prayed for relatives whose lives were in ruins. One man wrote from prison, saying that he was innocent and wanted to be home with his family. A teenage girl poured out her mistakes, begging God to forgive her.

Every written heart-cry had been unattended to, and was washed up on the beach.

Do you feel that God has thrown out your prayers? The Bible assures us that God hears and answers, even when we feel like no one else is listening. For followers of Jesus Christ, no prayer brought to God in the name of Jesus goes unanswered. Be encouraged; God is faithful. He may answer "yes" or maybe "no." He may say, "Wait," or perhaps "I've got something better." But He will answer.

Lord, even when I don't yet see Your answer, thank You for hearing my prayers and for faithfully answering me when I call to You.

Week 38 · Monday

HOW WILL THEY HEAR?

How then will they call on Him in whom they have not believed? And how are they to believe in Him of whom they have never heard? And how are they to hear without someone preaching? And how are they to preach unless they are sent? As it is written, "How beautiful are the feet of those who preach the good news!"

Romans 10:14-15

Tilly Smith, a ten-year-old girl from Great Britain, was vacationing with her family on a beach in Thailand.[3] As she played in the sand near the waves, the water bubbled and receded far from the shore. Tilly was petrified. She had learned in school about tsunamis, and realized what was happening. Tilly shouted, "Mommy, we've got to leave right now. I think there's going to be a tsunami."

No one understood until Tilly said "tidal wave." They hurriedly evacuated the area before the ocean water surged over the beach, demolishing everything in its path. No one at that beach was killed or seriously injured. More than one hundred people were saved because they believed the little girl's message.

That's how the gospel works. You know and share the message of Jesus, and lost people hear and believe that message. It's a message worth sharing. It's a message worth believing.

The Bible says judgment is coming. Hell awaits those without Jesus. The Bible says that Jesus died to save sinners, and that He offers eternal life to everyone who trusts in Him. Have you believed that message? Who will you share it with today?

Father, help me to share the gospel with urgency so people can be saved before it's too late!

Week 38   Tuesday

GET OUT OF THERE!

And when He rose from prayer, He came to the disciples and found them sleeping for sorrow, and He said to them, "Why are you sleeping? Rise and pray that you may not enter into temptation."

LUKE 22:45-46

There's an old saying that death and taxes are the only two guarantees in life. But there's a third, and it can prove to be more devastating than either death or taxes! What is it? Temptation.

"Temptation" has almost lost its negative connotation in today's culture. We casually talk about being tempted by fairly insignificant things like chocolate, or potato chips, or a really good sale at the mall. But temptation to sin is no light matter.

Temptation makes us keenly aware of what we think will satisfy us and make us happy. And just like custom-tailored suit, temptation is custom designed to fit your individual weaknesses, making it even more difficult to overcome!

Perhaps you're thinking right now about a temptation that you face regularly. You may already be feeling defeated. God wants you to be encouraged today! You are certainly not the only person to ever face temptation, and Satan will try to make you believe it's impossible to escape it.

God has promised to provide a way of escape. No temptation that comes to you is greater than the grace God gives to escape it. So look for the way of escape, and then take it!

Lord, help me to be aware of the many ways I am tempted every day. Thank You for making a way for me to escape temptation.

Week 38   Wednesday

STEEPING PROCESS

This Book of the Law shall not depart from your mouth, but you shall meditate on it day and night, so that you may be careful to do according to all that is written in it. For then you will make your way prosperous, and then you will have good success.

Joshua 1:8

Some people just love a good hot cup of tea. Around the world, tea drinkers have their favorite type of tea leaf, and their favorite addition: sugar, lemon, milk, cream, or cinnamon. One thing is true of every cup of tea. It is only made when tea leaves are steeped, infusing their flavor into the water.

The strength of the tea's flavor is determined by the length of time the leaves are left immersed in the water. A common tea bag steeped for thirty seconds will produce a very weak, bland cup of tea. But if you steep the tea for three to five minutes, your tea will taste like tea is supposed to taste.

The length of time we spend in God's Word determines how deeply we are changed by it. The more time we spend reading, studying, and praying over God's Word, the more our lives are flavored by it.

I challenge you to spend at least fifteen minutes every day reading and applying God's Word to your life. Memorize portions of the Bible. Meditate on it throughout the day. The more you are in the Word, the more the Word will be in you, and the more spiritually successful your life will be.

Thank You, God, that knowing and obeying Your Word will give me spiritual success.

Week 38   Thursday

LIGHTNING APPLAUSE

The Heavens declare the glory of God, and the sky above proclaims His handiwork. Day to day pours out speech, and night to night reveals knowledge. There is no speech, nor are there words, whose voice is not heard.

Psalm 19:1–3

Nikola Tesla invented the method of generating electricity through alternating current. It is said that during storms, Tesla burst into applause at lightning strikes – one genius recognizing the work of an even greater Genius! Tesla could appreciate the wonder of lightning because he had spent years researching and learning the wonders of electricity.

In the same way, the more we understand of God's world and God's Word, the more we appreciate the glory of our Creator.

Whether we see God's handiwork in the intricacy of a spider-web, the milky spiral of the Andromeda galaxy, the stirring beauty of Psalm 23, or the profound simplicity of John 3:16 – the longer we look at what God has done and said, the more deeply we praise His name!

Today, take a moment to meditate on some aspect of God's creation and upon a portion of His Word. As you do, don't neglect to gaze for a few moments upon the greatest work of God – the sacrificial death of His Son for your sins upon the cross of Calvary.

The greatness of God deserves more than our applause. He merits our unending awe, worship, faith, and obedience.

Father, You are an amazing God. Thank You for Your awesome creation that speaks of how wonderful You are.

Week 38   Friday

SELF-EXAMINATION

Examine yourselves, to see whether you are in the faith. Test yourselves. Or do you not realize this about yourselves, that Jesus Christ is in you?—unless indeed you fail to meet the test!
2 Corinthians 13:5

Several years ago, a man who wanted a great parking space at a New York Yankees baseball game pulled his car into the VIP lot and casually told the attendant that he was a friend of George Steinbrenner, the renowned owner of the Yankees.

Unfortunately for the imposter, the person attending the parking lot that day was George Steinbrenner himself! In a moment, the surprised imposter recognized Steinbrenner and stammered, "Guess I've got the wrong lot." He didn't park in the VIP lot that day, or ever.

The Bible says that God examines our hearts and knows all about us. He knows who His friends are and who the imposters are. As well, we need an honest self-examination to see if we are in agreement with God's evaluation of our hearts.

It's good to honestly examine ourselves to make sure we actually know Jesus Christ. Genuine times of examination do not produce doubt. Instead, asking whether we truly know Jesus will either produce a greater assurance of our salvation, or the opportunity for repentance and faith leading to eternal life.

Father, help me to honestly examine my heart to see if I belong to You.

Week 39   Monday

MERCY

Return to the Lord your God, for He is gracious and merciful, slow to anger, and abounding in steadfast love; and He relents over disaster.

Joel 2:13

A mother once approached French Emperor Napoleon Bonaparte seeking a pardon for her son.

The emperor replied that the young man had committed a certain offense twice and that justice demanded his death.

"But I don't ask for justice," the mother explained. "I plead for mercy."

"Your son does not deserve mercy," Napoleon replied.

"Sir," the woman cried, "it would not be mercy if he deserved it, and mercy is all I ask for."

The woman found mercy for her son; Napoleon spared his life.

We are all sinners. God's holiness demands that sin be paid for. However, God showed His great mercy for us at the cross of Jesus Christ. He doesn't desire that any should perish, but that we trust Jesus Christ and receive His mercy for our sin.

When we come to God with sorrow for our sin, trusting that Jesus Christ has paid its penalty in our place on the cross, we will find God merciful. We find His mercy when we first trust Christ for salvation, and for every sin we commit after that.

I am so thankful that God's mercy knows no limits. Aren't you?

Father, without Your mercy I would be lost forever. Thank You for having mercy on my soul!

191

Week 39   Tuesday

BASIC FUNDAMENTALS

Now I would remind you, brothers, of the gospel I preached to you, which you received, in which you stand, and by which you are being saved, if you hold fast to the word I preached to you—unless you believed in vain. For I delivered to you as of first importance what I also received: that Christ died for our sins in accordance with the Scriptures, that He was buried, that He was raised on the third day in accordance with the Scriptures.

1 Corinthians 15:1-4

Legendary basketball coach John Wooden always began the first practice of the season by teaching his players, very carefully, how to put on their socks. The lesson was repeated at the beginning of every practice, at the beginning of every game, for the entire season, every season. Why would he spend so much time on something so seemingly unimportant?

Coach Wooden had discovered that many players did not smooth out the wrinkles in their socks. Uncorrected, those wrinkles would cause blisters that would hamper their performance at crucial times during the games. The most basic fundamentals of the game are of absolute importance.

Of primary importance to every Christian is the pure gospel of Jesus Christ: He died, He was buried, and He rose from the dead. That foundational truth alone has the power to save every person from sin.

We can become so spiritually busy that we forget the gospel. Don't ever become so spiritually "mature" that the gospel loses its luster to you. Overlooking that fundamental truth will cause spiritual blisters that will trip you up in the race you are running for Jesus Christ. Never forget the fundamentals!

Lord, help me to never forget the beauty of the gospel and its importance in my life.

192

Week 39   Wednesday

GREAT PLANS

For I know the plans I have for you, declares the Lord, plans for welfare and not for evil, to give you a future and a hope.
                                                    Jeremiah 29:11

Ravi Zacharias tells a story of watching a father and son as they were weaving an Indian wedding garment known as a sari.[4]

He describes the process: The father sits on a platform, while the son sits below, surrounded by spools of thread. At the command of his father, the son moves the shuttle back and forth through the loom.

As the father leads and the son follows, eventually a beautiful design begins to appear.

It is interesting to note that the son works below the father, with only the reverse side of the emerging design visible to him. Only the father is able to see the beauty of the design as it is being woven. The son must patiently wait until the garment is complete before he can appreciate the father's design. He must follow the father's instructions and trust completely in the father's skill.

From the son's perspective, things look messy. From the father's perspective, there's a plan.

One day you will see the finished design of the life God is weaving in you. Until then, wait patiently and trust the Father's plan. He is making something beautiful of your life.

Father, though I cannot always see the entire plan You have for my life, I know Your plan is very good. Help me trust You when I cannot see.

Week 39   Thursday

GOD'S ANGER

In the eighth month, in the second year of Darius, the word of the Lord came to the prophet Zechariah, the son of Berechiah, son of Iddo, saying, "The Lord was very angry with your fathers. Therefore say to them, Thus declares the Lord of hosts: Return to Me, says the Lord of hosts, and I will return to you, says the Lord of hosts."

Zechariah 1:1-3

If you ever go to a show that features trained ocean animals, you have to be careful where you sit. Seats closest to the pool are in the "splash zone." When the animals crash into the water after leaping high into the air, those sitting in the "splash zone" get wet, even soaked. But, they can't say they weren't warned. There are always signs clearly marking the "splash zone."

God is holy and has righteous anger over our sin. Our sin places us in God's "anger zone." If we refuse to repent from our sin and return to God, we will stay in the "anger zone."

But God, in His wonderful mercy, has extended His forgiveness to us by sending His Son, Jesus Christ, to die on the cross and absorb His wrath for sin in our place. When we trust Jesus Christ to save us, He brings us out of the "anger zone."

The Bible gives us a clear warning that sin must be paid for. Jesus Christ paid for your sin on the cross so you could be forgiven and come out of God's anger zone. I pray you will trust Jesus today.

Father, I praise You for removing Your anger from me when I trusted Jesus as my Savior. Help me to warn others so they may be saved.

Week 39

A Heaven with No Jesus?

His divine power has granted to us all things that pertain to life and godliness, through the knowledge of Him who called us to His own glory and excellence.

2 Peter 1:3

What image comes to mind when you think of Heaven? Reunion with departed loved ones? No more sorrow or sickness? Streets of gold? No night? Unending peace? Let's see: have I forgotten anything? Oh yes...Jesus. Where is Jesus in your picture of Heaven?

We often talk, think, and sing about Heaven without any reference to Jesus. We look forward to seeing our loved ones or being free from pain and sorrow. Those things about Heaven seem to be the big draw for us.

Additionally, we often seek Jesus for the blessings He provides: a better marriage, a stronger family, peace and emotional stability, deliverance from harmful habits and addictions, or greater purpose and meaning in life. But do we seek Jesus simply for the joy of *knowing Jesus*?

Heaven is not primarily about being with our departed loved ones - though they will be there if they were believers - or walking on streets of gold - though the streets will be made of gold there. Heaven is preeminently about being with Jesus.

Jesus Christ will be what makes Heaven heavenly, and knowing Him makes life on earth worthwhile, as well!

Lord Jesus, thank You for Your presence with me here on earth, and thank You that I will be with You forever in Heaven!

Week 40

Monday

EGGS AND OMNISCIENCE

O Lord, You have searched me and known me! You know when I sit down and when I rise up; You discern my thoughts from afar.

Psalm 139:1-2

A small sea bird, the guillemot, lives on the rocky arctic cliffs of the northern coastal regions of North America. Thousands of guillemots will flock together in very small areas, where the females lay their pear-shaped eggs side by side in a long row on a very narrow ledge.

To human eyes, the eggs all look exactly alike. However, a mother guillemot can always identify her own eggs. Studies have shown that she knows her eggs so well that when even one is moved, she will find it and return it to its original location.

God is even more intimately acquainted with each of His children. There is absolutely nothing about your life that He does not know perfectly. He knows our every thought and our emotions. He is well-aware of each decision we must make and every problem we face.

He knows your name, your address, your telephone number, what you ate for breakfast this morning, and what you're most worried about right now. And, greater still, He loves you perfectly, with all the compassion of His holy heart.

Father, thank You that I am not hidden from Your sight. Thank You for being intimately aware of everything that concerns me.

Week 40 — Tuesday

COMPOUNDING JOY

For in a severe test of affliction, their abundance of joy and their extreme poverty have overflowed in a wealth of generosity on their part.

2 Corinthians 8:2

Long ago, people gathered to watch a world famous acrobat, named Blondin, confidently walk a tightrope across Niagara Falls and back. When he stepped from the rope back onto the ground, the crowd burst into wild applause.

Blondin addressed the admiring crowd. "Do you believe I can carry another person across the falls with me?" "Yes, we believe," the people replied. Then he issued an incredible invitation. "Who'll go with me? Will you let me take you across on my back?" he asked a man. No longer enthusiastic, the man timidly faded into the crowd. Man after man refused Blondin's invitation, until finally, one accepted. He climbed onto Blondin's back, and together they made it across the falls and back.

Everyone in the crowd that day said they believed. They acknowledged Blondin's ability to carry a man across the falls. Only one man trusted Blondin, and he demonstrated his trust by his actions.

Do your actions testify that you trust Jesus? A tangible way to demonstrate your trust is to give. Giving shows that you trust God to provide for you. Giving compounds the joy in our lives and builds greater faith.

Do you believe Jesus? Are you trusting Jesus?

Lord Jesus, help me to completely trust You when You ask me to walk with You in scary places.

Week 40   Wednesday

GUILT TRIP

If we confess our sins, He is faithful and just to forgive us our sins and to cleanse us from all unrighteousness.

1 John 1:9

Guilt is a miserable thing. But there's a difference between feeling guilty and being guilty. *Being guilty* is objective. It means we're responsible for doing something wrong, for sinning against God. But *feeling guilty* is subjective. It means we feel ashamed or embarrassed because of something we've done.

God and Satan are both interested in your guilt, but for very different reasons. God wants you to experience the guilt of your sin, so that you will come to Him in repentance. When you confess your sin, God forgives you, cleanses you from your unrighteousness, and restores you to a right relationship with Him.

Satan, on the other hand, wants you to experience unrelenting shame and embarrassment for your sin. He will lie to you that you are hopeless. In this way he can keep you down and defeated and of little use in God's kingdom.

If you are guilty, then repent of your sin and let God restore you through Christ. God's plan for His people is always to restore, always to forgive. When we confess our sin, He is faithful and just to forgive us our sin. God's forgiveness never comes with a side of guilt.

Father, thank You for removing the guilt of my sin. When I am guilty, help me confess quickly and receive Your complete forgiveness.

Week 40 — Thursday

HE KNOWS YOUR FRAME

For He knows our frame; He remembers that we are dust.
Psalm 103:14

Take a drive to the grocery store and you're likely to see heavy duty trucks in the parking lot. They're not just for construction workers and farmers anymore.

Engineers design truck frames for different purposes. For instance, the same truck you use to haul your groceries home might not have a strong enough frame to haul tons of concrete. A farm truck used to transport produce to the market might not be strong enough to tow heavy equipment to a construction site.

God designed us and He never forgets what He used to make us. He didn't use gold or precious jewels to fashion His highest creation. He used common dust. He gave us no strength or beauty of our own. Why? Because He designed us to need Him.

Only God's Spirit living inside us makes us strong to bear the loads of life's ups and downs. God in us overcomes our weaknesses, and empowers us to live in a way that pleases Him and brings glory to Jesus Christ.

Your body and your emotions may fail; they are just dust! But God will never fail you. He will be your strength and He is enough for your every need.

Father, I need You. I cannot bear the burdens of this life without You. Thank You that You are my strength!

Week 40

Friday

A One-Talent Superhero

His master said to him, "Well done, good and faithful servant. You have been faithful over a little; I will set you over much. Enter into the joy of your master."

Matthew 25:23

No two super heroes are alike. Take the Flash, for instance. The Flash is an amazing runner. That's all he does. He doesn't stop trains or freeze oceans. He runs. He's a one-talent superhero.

Superman is at least a five-talent super hero. He's faster than a speeding bullet, more powerful than a locomotive, can leap tall buildings in a single bound, has x-ray vision, and he's bullet-proof.

Do you think the Flash sulks because he has only one talent and Superman has at least five? Not according to the comic books. When there's trouble, the Flash dons his super hero costume and off he goes, running like the wind to help, and happy to do it.

If God has entrusted you with what seems like limited resources, understand this: What God has given you is very valuable. It is a great treasure and a wonderful inheritance. You are responsible, whether you have five-talents, two-talents, or one-talent, for being faithful with what God has given you.

Every day, be faithful with whatever God has entrusted to you, so that, when you are called into account on the last day, you will hear God will say of you, "Well done!"

Lord Jesus, help me to find great joy in serving You with the gifts and talents You have given me.

Week 41 — Monday

RETURNS ALLOWED

Therefore say to them, "Thus declares the Lord of hosts: Return to Me, says the Lord of hosts, and I will return to you, says the Lord of hosts."

Zechariah 1:3

Writing is part of what I do. I write articles, books, and sermons. I try to be careful to not overuse words, but sometimes it is necessary to use a particular word multiple times to make my point.

In the Bible, God uses words over and over to make His point to us. The word "return" is the twelfth most repeated word in the Old Testament. Sometimes it's translated "return." Sometimes it's translated "turn back." Sometimes it's translated "repent." God hammers His point home: He wants us to return to Him.

God's command to return to Him shows us that it is possible for us to make a U-turn, a total change of direction. He also makes a precious promise that when we return to Him, He will return to us. When you turn from your sin to God, you will find that He has already turned toward you.

When you feel the burden of your sin, and you realize you are far from God, remember His invitation. He loves you, and He wants you to return so you can be forgiven and be restored to Him.

Father, thank You that when we rebel against You, or when we wander far from You, You always desire that we return to You. Thank You for offering mercy and forgiveness to me when I sin.

Week 41   Tuesday

WASHING DISHES

You leave the commandment of God and hold to the tradition of men.

Mark 7:8

It's interesting to watch a child wash dishes. Most little ones will work very hard to get every speck of dirt off the outside of the cereal bowl, but they will totally ignore the inside, still plastered with dried cereal and milk. It's always the inside that needs a good scrubbing.

The Pharisees took great pains to create the appearance of holiness. They carefully followed a long, impressive list of rituals and traditions to look clean on the outside. However, their hearts remained dirty on the inside.

Traditions can be powerful aids to worship, but keeping them never earns favor with God. Without the blood of Jesus Christ removing sin from our hearts, we are just like a clumsy toddler, meticulously wiping the outside of the bowl but leaving the inside caked with gunk and grime.

Only a saving relationship with the Lord Jesus Christ can make our lives acceptable to God. His cleansing is a work of grace, and washes away every stain. Are you trying to earn God's favor by keeping rules and regulations, or are you trusting Christ alone to cleanse you completely of your sin?

I can't make myself clean, Lord. You alone can wash away the stain of my sin. Thank You, Jesus, that Your blood washes my sin away!

Week 41 Wednesday

MY BEST?

For we must all appear before the judgment seat of Christ, so that each one may receive what is due for what he has done in the body, whether good or evil.

2 Corinthians 5:10

In 1860, a steamship, carrying hundreds of sight-seers on Lake Michigan, collided with a schooner at two in the morning. Most aboard the ship died. Only a handful of passengers reached the lifeboats. But seventeen were saved by a college student named Edward Spencer.

Tethered to the shore by a rope around his waist, Edward swam through the waves time after time to grab exhausted victims clutching floating debris. Friends on the shore pulled at the rope to tow them to safety. Finally, badly fatigued and wounded, Spencer passed out. When he awoke in his room, his anguished question to his brother was, "Did I do my full duty? Did I do my best?"

Jesus Christ gives every Christian spiritual gifts, talents, and physical resources to use for His glory and to build His kingdom. He empowers us with His Holy Spirit to do everything He asks of us. We are to give Him our very best as we serve Him daily.

So as you encounter the opportunities the Lord gives you to serve Him today, ask yourself this simple, but life-changing question: Am I doing my very best to serve Jesus?

I know I will appear before Your judgment seat one day. Lord Jesus, help me to serve You the very best I know how by the power of the Holy Spirit so my life is pleasing to You.

203

Week 41   Thursday

SAND SCULPTURES

Now if anyone builds on the foundation with gold, silver, precious stones, wood, hay, straw—each one's work will become manifest, for the Day will disclose it, because it will be revealed by fire, and the fire will test what sort of work each one has done. If the work that anyone has built on the foundation survives, he will receive a reward. If anyone's work is burned up, he will suffer loss, though he himself will be saved, but only as through fire.

1 Corinthians 3:12-15

Many coastal cities host sand sculpture competitions. From a distance, these amazing works of art appear to be made of stone. But poking a sand sculpture with your finger can create significant damage. Even worse, when the rain comes or the waves get too close, the sculpture washes away. It seems like a lot of effort for something that's gone with the next downpour.

If you want the life you build to have significance that will last, it must be built upon the foundation of Jesus Christ, and constructed of works with the lasting power of gold, silver, and precious stones. Jesus Christ will judge our works, the Bible says, by fire. No matter how skillfully or beautifully you build your life, if it is not in obedience to Jesus Christ and for His glory, it will not stand.

What a waste to present to Jesus a life for which there will be no reward. If you are living to serve Jesus and bring Him glory, He will supply all the building materials you need to construct a life that will survive the fire of judgment and that He can reward.

I want my life to be eternally significant, Lord! Help every effort of my life to bring You glory, so that I am not ashamed when I stand before You.

204

Week 41   Friday

SELF-DECEPTION

I acknowledged my sin to You, and I did not cover my iniquity; I said, "I will confess my transgressions to the Lord," and You forgave the iniquity of my sin.

Psalm 32:5

A Sunday school teacher asked the children around her table, "Can anyone tell me what you must do to be forgiven of your sin?" After a moment, from the back of the room, a small boy spoke up with an innocent, but obvious answer. "Sin," he said. His answer was innocent, but we're obviously all guilty.

Satan has a dangerous plot to make us feel okay when we're not. He wants us to feel innocent when we're guilty, and clean when we're dirty so we'll continue in the sin that's destroying us.

God's Word warns us against this type of self-deception. The Bible is God's unchanging standard. Sinful behavior that is acceptable in our culture is not acceptable to God. Sexual relationships apart from the marriage of one man and one woman are sin. Lying is always wrong. Cheating is always sinful.

Don't sweep under the rug or rationalize the feeling of conviction that comes with your sin. Conviction is God's tool to bring you back to Him in repentance so you can receive His forgiveness through Jesus Christ.

Remember, when it comes to your guilt, Satan will always deceive you, and God will always tell you the truth.

Your word is truth and is my standard for living, Lord. Help me to always agree with You about my sin, even if the world says I'm okay.

Week 42 — Monday

JESUS CHANGES EVERYTHING

But now you must put them all away: anger, wrath, malice, slander, and obscene talk from your mouth. Do not lie to one another, seeing that you have put off the old self with its practices and have put on the new self, which is being renewed in knowledge after the image of its Creator.

Colossians 3:8-9

What would you like to change about yourself? Many people desperately want to change how they look, hoping that it will change how they feel on the inside. Can you identify?

Superficial changes may alter our look, but they don't change us. The only way for us to truly be changed is to be changed from the inside out by someone greater than us. That's what Jesus does.

We most often think of the change Jesus makes in our destination. When He saves us, we are no longer headed for Hell. Instead, our eternal home will be in Heaven with Him! But Jesus changes much more than that. When Jesus is Lord of your life, He changes your ambitions, your outlook, your reputation, and your loyalties. He changes your language and your passions. You gradually lose your resemblance to the old you, and begin to look more and more like Jesus.

Have you been changed, or do you still look and sound like the old you? If there is no change in your life, there is no Jesus in your life. But if Jesus is in your life, you can't stay the same, because Jesus changes everything!

Lord, help me to put away the sinful behavior that You've forgiven, and instead display the character of Jesus in my life.

Week 42 — Tuesday

PICNICS AND FUNERALS

Hear, O Lord, and be merciful to me! O Lord, be my helper! You have turned for me my mourning into dancing; You have loosed my sackcloth and clothed me with gladness, that my glory may sing Your praise and not be silent. O Lord my God, I will give thanks to You forever!

Psalm 30:10-12

A few years ago, Michele and I attended a picnic for preschoolers and their families on our church campus. We joined dads and moms sitting on blankets on the ground, joyfully watching the children run and play games. There were lots of smiles and laughter.

In about an hour a group of people wearing dark suits and dresses walked past us on the sidewalk, headed for a funeral inside. In contrast to the laughter of our picnic, they were very somber and subdued.

We did our best to quiet things down for a few moments in respect of the mourners. But the children continued to laugh and play. After all, it *was* a picnic.

That scene is a great reminder that when you're enjoying a picnic, someone else is grieving. When you're mourning a loss, someone else is laughing and playing. When you're celebrating life's greatest joys, someone else is experiencing their greatest sorrow.

Whether you are having a picnic day or a funeral day, you can give thanks to the Lord and sing His praise. He meets our deepest needs when we experience the extremes of life. God is always with us, in every kind of situation. Praise the Lord!

Thank You, Father, that You are with me at all times, in my joys and in my sorrows.

Week 42   Wednesday

A GOOD NAME

A good name is to be chosen rather than great riches, and favor is better than silver or gold.

Proverbs 22:1

In high school, I took one class that I've used every day of my life since: typing. In those days, we used old-fashioned Royal typewriters. A typewriter works like this: you strike the letter keys, which in turn move the type bar. The type bar strikes an ink ribbon, and the ink ribbon leaves the impression of the letters on the paper behind it. The marks left on the paper are simply the impressions of the letters on the type bars.

You leave an impression on every person you meet. What do people think about when they hear your name? Followers of Jesus Christ will have a reputation that reflects His character.

Reputation is not the same as character. Character is what God knows about you. He knows who you really are because He knows your heart, even better than you know it. Your reputation is what other people think about you. If you have a godly character, you will have a good reputation.

The Bible says that a good name, a good reputation, is more valuable than gold. What value does your name carry? Does the mark you leave show you are a Christ follower?

I want my reputation to be one that brings glory to You, Father! Help me to leave the impression of Jesus on people I deal with today.

Week 42   Thursday

THE WORLD OR GOD'S WILL?

Do not love the world or the things in the world. If anyone loves the world, the love of the Father is not in him. For all that is in the world —the desires of the flesh and the desires of the eyes and pride of life — is not from the Father but is from the world. And the world is passing away along with its desires, but whoever does the will of God abides forever.

1 John 2:15-17

Boxing legend Muhammed Ali is arguably one of the greatest and most popular athletes of all time. In addition, he was also a superb entertainer. He could keep an opponent on the ropes and a crowd in stitches. His face appeared on the cover of *Sports Illustrated* more times than any other athlete.

Only a few years after retirement, Ali's body was beset with Parkinson's disease. His celebrity slowly faded. Sportswriter Gary Smith visited Ali at his farmhouse. The former boxer took Smith on a tour of his barn, where photos of Ali in his prime lined the walls. Ali turned each photo toward the wall.

"I had the world," he said, "and it wasn't nothin'. Look now."

The world is temporary. Its fame, pleasures, and wealth are all passing away. Whatever material things we're holding onto, regardless of their current value and beauty, will one day be gone. They could be gone tomorrow.

If our priorities are in short-lived things, we will inevitably wind up disappointed. God's will, however, is unchanging and eternal. Those who follow Him will reap an eternal and unfading reward.

Help me to live not for the things that are passing away, Lord, but for the imperishable things You have reserved for me in Heaven. Help me to do Your will today.

Week 42

Friday

NICE CAMERA!

For although they knew God, they did not honor Him as God or give thanks to Him, but they became futile in their thinking, and their foolish hearts were darkened.

Romans 1:21

A man took hundreds of pictures while on vacation with his wife. She shared them with her friends and co-workers when they got back. Invariably, people would respond, "Wow, your husband must have a really nice camera!"

These comments disappointed her husband. He complained, "Nobody looks at a painting and says, 'Nice brushes!' Nobody looks at a sculpture and says, 'Nice chisel!' Why doesn't someone say, 'He's a great photographer?' "

His wife asked, "So, how often do you look at creation and say, 'Nice work, God?' "

We are prone to only be thankful for God's blessings instead of giving thanks to God Himself. How often do you stop to praise God for His goodness and His mighty deeds? When we see the glory of God's creation, or when we experience the joy of His goodness and faithfulness to us, we must look beyond the blessing to the One who blesses. We must see beyond the creation to the Creator.

Thanking God for what He has done brings us into closer relationship with Him. Don't be more thankful for your blessings than for God who blesses!

Lord, You are glorious, merciful, and kind! Thank You that every blessing from Your hand tells of Your goodness!

Week 43

Monday

IDOLS? NOT HERE!

For they themselves report concerning us the kind of reception we had among you, and how you turned to God from idols to serve the living and true God.

1 Thessalonians 1:9

Carved idols have been worshiped throughout history in many cultures. Once, when I was waiting to preach at a church in Malaysia, I perused the bulletin, where this announcement caught my attention: "Idol Removal Service," followed by the place and the time.

I asked the pastor about it. He said that, in their church, people come to Jesus Christ from a life of idol worship. When they get saved, they bring their idol statue to the curb, smash it to pieces, and leave it with the trash. In a very literal sense, they turn from useless idols to faith in Jesus Christ.

But idols are not only those that are made of wood or metal. The Hebrew word for "idol" means "an empty thing." We often allow empty things to occupy the place in our hearts that only Jesus should occupy. It may be your job, or your money. It might be pleasure. Perhaps it's a relationship with another person. We can even idolize ourselves.

Are you serving an idol today instead of serving Jesus Christ? Don't let empty things rob you of your relationship with the living and true God.

Search my heart today to see if I am worshiping empty things, Father. Help me to get rid of any idol that I allow to occupy Your place in my life.

Week 43   Tuesday

AN AWESOME GOD

*And I heard every creature in Heaven and on earth and under
the earth and in the sea, and all that is in them, saying, "To
Him who sits on the throne and to the Lamb be blessing and
honor and glory and might forever and ever!"*

Revelation 5:13

I'll never forget the first time Michele and I visited the Grand
Canyon. As we gazed across that huge chasm, we were
fascinated, awestruck, and inspired by the handiwork of God
on display there. It was almost impossible to look away.

So it is with the splendor, the wonder, and the beauty of our
Lord Jesus Christ.

Revelation 1:13-16 describes our glorified Lord: "In the midst
of the lampstands one like a Son of Man, clothed with a long
robe and with a golden sash around His chest. The hairs of
His head were white, like white wool, like snow. His eyes were
like a flame of fire, His feet were like burnished bronze,
refined in a furnace, and His voice was like the roar of many
waters. In His right hand He held seven stars, from His mouth
came a sharp two-edged sword, and His face was like the sun
shining in full strength."

The majesty of our Lord should cause us to fall before Him in
worship, gladly surrendering our lives to Him. Today, take
time to draw near to God, to gaze upon His holiness, and
experience the power of His presence in your life.

---

*Sometimes I forget how powerful and glorious You are, Jesus. I
worship You! There is no one higher or more powerful than You!*

Week 43 — Wednesday

DREAM-KILLERS

His brothers said to him, "Are you indeed to reign over us? Or are you indeed to rule over us?" So they hated him even more for his dreams and for his words.

Genesis 37:8

A *Peanuts* cartoon showed Snoopy joyfully sliding along a frozen pond on his little bare paws. Then Lucy glides out onto the pond in her skates. As Snoopy does a happy little twirl, Lucy haughtily lectures him, "That's not skating, that's just sliding."

Snoopy lowers his head, thinking, "I thought I was having fun."

We're all faced with dream-killers. Joseph's brothers tried to kill his dream, and even considered killing him! But Joseph's dream had been given by God, and nothing could kill what God would do through Joseph. Though sold into slavery by his brothers, and wrongfully imprisoned in Egypt for years, Joseph remained faithful to God. He became the prime minister of Egypt, and saved the nation and his own family during a time of severe famine in the land.

Don't give up on any dream God places in your heart. Trust God's Word and don't grow tired of Scripture's simple truths. Never forget how much God loves you and how He desires to use you to share the gospel and advance His kingdom.

Place yourself and your dream in God's hands. If He has given you the dream, He will bring it to pass.

I thank You, Father, that every plan of Yours will come to pass. Help me to be faithful to pursue any dream You place in my heart.

Week 43   Thursday

YOUR SPIRITUAL HEALTH

My son, give attention to my words; incline your ear to my sayings. Do not let them depart from your eyes; keep them in the midst of your heart; for they are life to those who find them, and health to all their flesh.

Proverbs 4:20-22

As a child, my mom and dad guarded over my physical health. They made sure I had good food to eat, spent time playing in the fresh air, got to bed on time so I'd be alert the next day, and took me to the doctor for regular checkups.

As an adult, I still try to live by the guidelines for good health that my parents taught me. These same guidelines for physical health can also be applied to maintaining spiritual health for a child of God:

Daily Food – Take in the "pure milk of the word" through study and meditation.

Fresh Air – Pray often. Prayer is the oxygen of the soul.

Regular Exercise – Obey what you learn in God's Word.

Adequate Rest – Rely on God at all times in simple faith.

Clean Surroundings – Avoid evil company and whatever will weaken you spiritually.

Loving Care – Be part of a church where you will benefit from a pastor's teaching and Christian fellowship.

Periodic Checkups – Regularly examine your spiritual health.

Lord, help me to guard over the health of my spiritual life with as much attention as I do the health of my physical body.

Week 43   Friday

REMEMBER

And when He had given thanks, He broke it, and said, "This is My body which is for you. Do this in remembrance of Me." In the same way also He took the cup, after supper, saying, "This cup is the new covenant in My blood. Do this, as often as you drink it, in remembrance of Me." For as often as you eat this bread and drink the cup, you proclaim the Lord's death until He comes.

1 Corinthians 11:24-26

Many people experience tragedy in their lives, often leaving them with painful memories and the continued grief of great loss. Although the passing of time can ease the pain of loss, when reminders come, emotions often come flooding back.

On the night before Jesus went to the cross, He shared the Passover meal with His disciples. As He broke the bread to share with them and passed the cup, He instructed them that every time they partook of this meal in the future, they should do it "in remembrance of Me."

We should never let the communion service become a mere formality. It should always be a tender and touching experience, reminding us that the body of the Lord Jesus was painfully broken for us, and His blood spilled for the payment of our sin. Every time we partake, we are reminded of His sacrificial death.

There is also joy in remembering, because it is a proclamation that Jesus is coming again! The death of Jesus Christ wasn't final because He victoriously rose from the grave on the third day. That gives us hope that we will see Him again, and also our loved ones who trusted Jesus.

My salvation cost You everything, Lord. Never let me forget the great sacrifice You made so I could live with You forever.

Week 44　　　　　Monday

HUNGER FOR GOD

O God, You are my God; earnestly I seek You; my soul thirsts for You; my flesh faints for You, as in a dry and weary land where there is no water.

Psalm 63:1

Have you ever been walking through the shopping mall when suddenly you get a whiff of cinnamon? You were just minding your own business, but now these drifting molecules of sugar, butter, and spice collide with a susceptible patch inside your nose.

Now you *want* a cinnamon roll. Your mouth starts to salivate. Your stomach begins to ache for it. This yearning for a cinnamon roll is real. You've had an *encounter* with a cinnamon roll in the past. Past experience tells you how good they are. You want it again.

What if you try to satisfy your desire for a warm, comforting cinnamon roll with something else, like a piece of cinnamon gum? You can try, but it's just not the same. You have your cinnamon candy; I'm having a cinnamon roll!

Don't try to satisfy your longings with things that will never satisfy. The never-ending pursuit of satisfaction through television, video games, social media, money, sex, exercise, work, or relationships will never meet your deepest desires. We were created to be satisfied by God alone.

God wants to fill the deepest longings of your heart. Earnestly seek Him.

Lord, life is dry and weary when I am not seeking You. Please fill my heart today with Your presence and Your power.

216

Week 44 — Tuesday

JEHOVAH JIREH

He said, "Do not lay your hand on the boy or do anything to him, for now I know that you fear God, seeing you have not withheld your son, your only son, from Me." And Abraham lifted up his eyes and looked, and behold, behind him was a ram, caught in a thicket by his horns. And Abraham went and took the ram and offered it up as a burnt offering instead of his son. So Abraham called the name of that place, "The Lord will provide"; as it is said to this day, "On the mount of the Lord it shall be provided."

Genesis 22:12-14

What do you need? I mean, what do you *really* need? Has God asked you to do something in His name that you just don't see a way to do? Has He asked you for something that you think is just too hard?

You can imagine how shocked, dismayed, and broken Abraham must have felt when God came to him, and, in a voice as clear as any he had ever heard, told Abraham to sacrifice his only son. What would Abraham do? This was the hardest test he had ever faced.

We know that Abraham passed the test. Just as he was about to thrust his knife into the chest of his precious son, God stopped him. In Isaac's place, God provided a ram for the sacrifice He required.

As Abraham obeyed God with absolutely all he had, God provided in an unexpected way, just in time, and in response to Abraham's radical and obedient faith. In the same way, when you place your faith in God for the tests and trials you encounter, He can work in ways you never imagined to provide just what you need, just when you need it!

Father, I trust You in my trial. Thank You for working for my good, building my faith, and helping me to have confidence in You.

Week 44   Wednesday

DELIVER US FROM EVIL

And lead us not into temptation, but deliver us from evil.

Matthew 6:13

In school, pop quizzes were a guarantee. If you had studied and had done your homework, being diligent to be prepared, then a pop quiz was an invitation to success. However, if you didn't study and tossed aside your homework, thinking you could cram for an exam at the last minute, then a pop quiz would pretty much ruin your day.

You don't know when temptation will come, but you know for sure that it will. The key to victory is to be prepared at all times. Stay in the Word of God daily. Confess your weaknesses to God and constantly rely upon the Holy Spirit of God to strengthen you, to help you recognize temptation, and to find the way of escape.

Satan, the tempter, is great at his job. One reason temptation feels so powerful is that he catches us off guard, dangling his lure when we least expect it, or when we're tired, or when we're stressed. We need to be prepared for those times.

You can't win over temptation on your own. With the power of God working in you and through you, you will be able to recognize temptation and escape from it when it arises!

I want to recognize temptation when it comes. Open my eyes, Lord, and strengthen my heart against the schemes of the devil.

Week 44 — Thursday

ABUNDANT LIFE

The thief does not come except to steal, and to kill, and to destroy. I have come that they may have life, and that they may have it more abundantly.

John 10:10

As we recognize a day of Thanksgiving, it's a good time to recall a speech given by President Franklin Roosevelt on December 6, 1933, as the Great Depression had the nation in its grip. Roosevelt spoke that day on the need for American families to be economically secure. He called his address: "The Right to More Abundant Life."

Most people think of abundance in terms of material possessions and the American dream: a home of your own, two cars in the garage, college for the kids, new clothes, food on the table, vacations, and money in the bank. Those abundant blessings, however, can disappear in a moment, as they did in the Great Depression.

Although every good thing comes to us from God's gracious hand, Jesus Christ came not to give abundant "stuff," but abundant life! Through Christ, God gives us abundant mercy, abundant provision, abundant kindness, abundant pardon, and abundant peace.

Don't ignore the abundance of the life you have in Christ. We can be thankful every day and have joy in the Lord because He gives to us abundantly to meet every need.

Forgive me for thinking that having abundant stuff is the same as abundant life! Lord, help me to seek the abundant life that You died to give me.

Week 44

Friday

TRAINING WHEELS

About this we have much to say, and it is hard to explain, since you have become dull of hearing. For though by this time you ought to be teachers, you need someone to teach you again the basic principles of the oracles of God. You need milk, not solid food, for everyone who lives on milk is unskilled in the word of righteousness, since he is a child. But solid food is for the mature, for those who have their powers of discernment trained by constant practice to distinguish good from evil.

Hebrews 5:11-14

I remember the day my dad bought me a brand new, red, white and blue bicycle. It had tall handlebars and a banana seat. I was thrilled, but I wobbled badly when I tried to ride it. So, Dad put the training wheels on for me.

For three weeks I had a great time riding my bike, because the training wheels made me feel safe. I didn't wobble with the training wheels. But in about three weeks, to my dismay, Dad came with his tools and removed the training wheels. I protested loudly. "I've got to, son," he said, "you've never really ridden a bicycle until you've ridden without the training wheels." And off they came.

God may be working right now to take the training wheels off of some area of your life. It is easy to become dependent on things like money, or other people, or routine. These things can make us feel comfortable, but finding our security in them will keep us from walking by faith and trusting in Jesus.

God knows what He's doing when He removes our training wheels. Trust Him for your security and joy each day. You're not really living unless you do!

God, when You ask me to trust You, I often feel wobbly. Help me to have confidence in You when You take away things I've trusted to make me feel secure.

Week 45 — Monday

THE PERFECT VIOLIN

Let not sin therefore reign in your mortal body, to make you obey its passions. Do not present your members to sin as instruments for unrighteousness, but present yourselves to God as those who have been brought from death to life, and your members to God as instruments for righteousness.

Romans 6:12-13

When violin maker Antonio Stradivari died in 1737, a particular violin was found in his studio. It had never been played. It has still never been played. This violin, called "The Messiah," was said to be the "perfect violin." Today, the Messiah is in a museum, the only instrument to have its own showcase.

How can the "perfect violin" remain unplayed? It cannot, according to Ivry Gitlis, a violinist who plays his Stradivarius every day. Of his violin, he says, "My violin was born in 1713. It is not my violin. Rather, I am its violinist; I am only passing through its life."

Each of us is an instrumental in the Messiah's symphony. Our purpose is to bring our lives into accord with desire of the Composer and the Conductor.

Wouldn't it be shameful if a trained artist positioned a Stradivarius under his chin, drew the bow across the strings and produced squeals and squeaks, rather than beautiful music he is capable of producing? As those brought from death to life, we have the power to be instruments of righteousness. Don't let the strains of sin be heard in your life. Instead, present your life to God to produce the beautiful melody of His righteousness.

I thank You that You have brought me from death to life. Lord, here is my life. Help me to live a godly life and not obey the passions of sin.

Week 45   Tuesday

IMMANUEL

The virgin will be pregnant and will give birth to a Son. They will name Him Immanuel. (Immanuel means "God with us.")

Matthew 1:23

An ancient Persian king loved his people so much that he would go out to mingle with them, carefully disguised to hide his royalty. One day, he went to the public baths, dressed as a very poor man. Beneath the baths was a huge furnace, tended by a man who kept the fires burning.

The disguised king and the furnace keeper spent time together every day for weeks. Finally, the king revealed himself. He imagined that the furnace keeper would ask something of him when he learned his true identity. However, amazingly, the man responded, "I want nothing from you. It's enough that you've shared my time and really cared for me. I don't want anything other than your company."

Jesus Christ left the royal halls of Heaven to come and live among us. He knows what it's like to hurt. He knows what it's like to be tempted, to struggle, to have His heart broken. He knows what it's like to be you.

He lived a perfect life, died a sacrificial death, and rose victoriously from the grave for the forgiveness of our sins. Through the Holy Spirit, He is with every person who trusts Him.

Thank You Jesus that You became a man and walked among us, died for our sin, and now live in Your people through Your Holy Spirit!

Week 45   Wednesday

SOUL CAGES

Put off your old self, which belongs to your former manner of life and is corrupt through deceitful desires, and to be renewed in the spirit of your minds, and ...put on the new self, created after the likeness of God in true righteousness and holiness.

Ephesians 4:22-24

A zoo received the gift of a beautiful polar bear. However, there was no appropriate area where the bear could reside. The zoo began construction of a wonderful polar bear habitat.

During construction, the bear was housed in a small temporary space where there was room for the bear to only take three steps, turn around, and walk three steps back.

Construction of the polar bear habitat took three years. When finally brought into his wonderfully spacious and beautiful new home, the bear looked around, took three steps, turned around, and took three steps back. The polar bear was still living in his past.

Followers of Jesus Christ are often tempted to practice the same habits, have the same attitudes, delve in the same sins, and follow the same mindset that we had before we were saved. Your enemy wants to keep you caged, bound by your former life.

In Christ you are a new creation, saved to live a life of righteousness and holiness. Don't be mastered by past sins and attitudes. You are not the same person you were. Let your mind be renewed and intentionally live the new life Christ has for you.

I am a new creation, not the same person I was before Jesus saved me. Father, help me make righteous choices and think righteous thoughts.

Week 45   Thursday

ARE YOU TICKLISH?

For the Word of God is living and active, sharper than any two-edged sword, piercing to the division of soul and of spirit, of joints and of marrow, and discerning the thoughts and intentions of the heart.

Hebrews 4:12

I'm very ticklish. In fact, if you just act like you're going tickle me, I'll turn and go the other way! But you know, I've never been able to tickle myself. I can poke myself in the ribs, and it's just a poke. If I swipe a feather across my own foot, I don't react at all.

Likewise, because we are sinful, we cannot evaluate our own hearts. But God can. The Holy Spirit of God uses the Word of God to reveal what is in our hearts. Then, we are responsible to obey what He shows us and bring our lives into agreement with His Word.

The Word of God will confirm our salvation – whether we are saved or not. It will reveal our deepest thoughts and the intentions of our hearts. It shows us our sin, and reveals God's desire for us. It's like a mirror, showing us what needs to be corrected and put in place.

We cannot please God without surrendering to the authority of His Word. Ask the Holy Spirit to search your heart with God's Word. The Bible not only reveals God to us, it reveals our own hearts to us.

Father, You know my thoughts and intentions. Use Your Word to reveal to me my true thoughts and intentions, so I can align them with Your desire for me.

Week 45 — Friday

STIR IT UP!

And let us consider how to stir up one another to love and good works, not neglecting to meet together, as is the habit of some, but encouraging one another, and all the more as you see the Day drawing near.

Hebrews 10:24-25

Who are you sharing recipes with? Are you helping someone improve their golf game? Who are you giving a ride to work or to school? Who are you helping to become more like Jesus? Who is helping you to become more like Jesus?

Of course, the most practical place for this to happen is in the local church. In Bible believing churches everywhere, there are people who will love you, hold you accountable, walk through the trials of life with you, and rejoice in God's blessings with you.

Too many times, however, people go to church, completely bypassing small groups where relationships are built. They create their own personal space in the worship service, never welcoming anyone in. They don't talk to anyone or pray with anyone. And when the service is over, they walk out, never having personally connected with anyone.

Don't neglect the great importance of really connecting with the body of Christ in the local church. If you are not currently part of a local church, finding a church home needs to be a priority for you. If you are part of a local church, I hope you are investing in others and letting them invest in you.

Father, help me to make relationships in the church body a priority. Make me an encouragement to someone at church this week.

Week 46   Monday

MORE EXCELLENT THINGS

And it is my prayer that your love may abound more and more, with knowledge and all discernment, so that you may approve what is excellent, and so be pure and blameless for the day of Christ, filled with the fruit of righteousness that comes through Jesus Christ, to the glory and praise of God.

Philippians 1:9-11

Prayer is the very best thing we can do for others. Most of us are eager to pray for others in crisis moments when finances, health, and relationships hang in the balance. But how do we pray for them when storms aren't brewing and the seas are calm?

The prayers of Paul for his friends are wonderful examples of how we can pray for one another. In the introduction of his letters, Paul always mentions how he is praying for his friends. His prayers for them touch levels of their lives that are much deeper than their immediate needs.

See what Paul prays in the above verses. He prays that their love (for Christ and others) will abound, for their knowledge and discernment to grow, that they will live with spiritual excellence so they will be pure and blameless when Jesus returns. He prays that they will bring glory to Christ by producing His fruit in their lives.

These are heart changing prayers! Your loved ones need God to be at work in their lives, every season and every day. Let's not limit our prayers to our physical needs. Let's pray for the more excellent things.

Teach me how to pray for spiritually excellent things for my friends and family, Lord.

Week 46   Tuesday

A HOLY HOUSEKEEPER

Flee from sexual immorality. Every other sin a person commits is outside the body, but the sexually immoral person sins against his own body. Or do you not know that your body is a temple of the Holy Spirit within you, whom you have from God? You are not your own, for you were bought with a price. So glorify God in your body.

1 Corinthians 6:18-20

Mom has worked hard all day to make the house spotless. Then the door flies open, and there stands a grimy five-year-old with nasty shoes. Mom cries, "Don't come in this house with those muddy shoes on!" He stops, parks the shoes by the door, and the house stays clean. Crisis averted!

The Holy Spirit of God lives inside every follower of Jesus Christ. When we are tempted by sexual sin, He's not going to be quiet about it. He's going to speak loudly and plainly, "Don't do that! This is going to dirty up my house!" He's not going to compromise or argue with you. He's just going to say, "Stop!"

The devil will speak up, too, with a voice of compromise. When you start to reason out why sexual sin is okay, or when you try to find a way around the Holy Spirit's "no," that's the enemy speaking, and it's a dangerous place to be.

Heeding God's voice will help us keep clean, pure hearts and protect us from mounds of guilt and painful consequences. Don't dirty God's dwelling place. Your body belongs to God. Run from sexual immorality and glorify God with your body.

Father, thank You for speaking loudly and clearly when I am tempted to commit sexual sin. Help me to listen and obey You quickly!

Week 46   Wednesday

ASK BIG

And I tell you, ask, and it will be given to you; seek, and you will find; knock, and it will be opened to you. For everyone who asks receives, and the one who seeks finds, and to the one who knocks it will be opened.

Luke 11:9-10

When Dr. Haddon Robinson was serving as president of the Denver Theological Seminary, he petitioned a local businessman for a financial contribution to help pay for a new phone system. The man asked, "How much will it cost?" Dr. Robinson replied, "About $20,000." "How much are you asking me for?" asked the man. "I'm asking you for $1000," replied Dr. Robinson.

The man slid a check for $1000 across the desk. "You have either underestimated my resources, or underestimated my generosity. You should have asked me for $20,000 and I would happily have given it. Never be afraid to ask big. The worst that can happen is that I'd have said no." Dr. Robinson left that day with $1000, but he learned a big lesson.

To *ask* means to pray with expectancy. Ask big things of God! God faithfully provides our needs, so we can ask for vastly greater things than material possessions. Ask God to display His glory in your life. Ask for the souls of lost people to be saved. Ask God to bring a spiritual awakening in our land. Don't limit your petitions of God. Ask, and it will be given to you.

Teach me to ask big, Lord! Show me what it means to ask for great things in Your name and for Your glory.

Week 46 — Thursday

BE A GOD PLEASER

Finally, then, brothers, we ask and urge you in the Lord Jesus, that as you received from us how you ought to walk and to please God, just as you are doing, that you do so more and more.

1 Thessalonians 4:1

Our grandmothers had what they jokingly called "Tennessee Tupperware", a haphazard collection of recycled margarine containers they used to store every leftover in the kitchen. If your grandmother sent you to get the margarine, it was always wise to look inside the tub. Even if the outside of the container was labeled "margarine," there was always a good chance it held yesterday's pot roast.

Just like grandmother's kitchen, Christians can be confused by the false labeling in today's culture. The world is quick to label things that are evil as "good," or things that are good as "evil."

Not wanting to appear unloving, some Christians accept this kind of moral reversal to please others. But calling pot roast "margarine" won't make you able to spread it on your toast. Just because man says something is good does not mean God agrees. And we must always accept God's ways as true and right when they conflict with man's ways.

The Bible clearly teaches us how we should walk to please God. If you are conflicted about a moral issue, you can count on God's Word to show you the way, every time. Live to be a God pleaser, not a world pleaser.

The world's ways are against Your ways, Father. Help me to live every moment to please You and not the world.

Week 46

A Bold AND Relational Witness

Whenever you enter a town and they receive you, eat what is set before you. Heal the sick in it and say to them, "The kingdom of God has come near to you."

Luke 10:8-9

In a small town where my family used to live, about once a month a group of people from a local church would gather at the main intersection. They held up signs with scriptures about salvation on them. Sometimes one of them would stand on the street corner and preach. They were bold in their witness, but they had no relationship. Most people just drove on by.

I also know people who have great relationships with unsaved people. They play golf with them. Perhaps their kids are in play groups together. At the end of the day they may think of you, "He's a really nice person!" But they are never bold enough to share the gospel with them.

We are sent by God to reach people for Christ. So do we build relationships? Of course. Do we pray for people and help them? Yes. But there also must be a bold witness that says, "The kingdom of God has come near to you. Jesus is coming, and you need to be saved."

Boldness without relationship is rarely effective. Relationship without boldness is rarely effective. But relationship and boldness will change people's lives.

Lord, give me opportunity in every relationship to share the gospel so people can be saved.

Week 47   Monday

FAITH FOR YOUR FEARS

Fear not, for I am with you; be not dismayed, for I am your God; I will strengthen you, I will help you, I will uphold you with My righteous right hand.

Isaiah 41:10

"I promise..." How many times have you begun a sentence with those two words? Do you always keep your promises? God does. Sometimes, we make promises that we are unable or even unwilling to keep, or we promise things that are unwise. That's not how it is with our God. Because He only tells the truth, and because His wisdom, power, and love are so great, God keeps each promise He ever makes.

God promises to help you when you are afraid. He speaks with a strong, reassuring voice and says, "Don't be afraid. Don't be discouraged. I will strengthen you and help you." The unpredictability of life, financial setbacks, physical illness, prolonged suffering, and loneliness are just a few of the factors that may make you afraid. When you face these problems by yourself, you can become paralyzed by fear.

Someone has wisely observed that you cannot break God's promises by leaning on them! God offers promises, faith trusts those promises, and prayer claims them. When you pray during times of fear, God will make you strong.

If you are encountering fear today, you can lean on God's promise for strength and help.

Father, thank You that Your promises never break. Teach me to trust in You today and not to be afraid.

Week 47   Tuesday

WARNING LABELS

For the love of money is a root of all kinds of evils. It is through this craving that some have wandered away from the faith and pierced themselves with many pangs.

1 Timothy 6:10

Did you know your deodorant has a warning label that reads, "Warning: For external use only." Deodorant seems harmless, and it is a helpful, and even a necessary thing. But it can be misused, causing great harm.

Money on its own seems harmless. It's just metal or paper, after all. Money is necessary, and a blessing. But it is potentially very dangerous. We must be very vigilant to use it the right way. The Bible carries money's warning label.

All of what scripture teaches about money can be boiled down to two truths. First, money, wealth, and possessions are all blessings from the Lord. It's not a sin to be wealthy. It is God who gives wealth.

But an equally important truth is that money can consume and destroy us when it begins to possess the affections of our hearts. The love of money even causes some to stray from their faith in Jesus Christ because of greediness. The love of money harms reputations and relationships, bringing many sorrows.

Do you have a love for money? Are you greedy? Thank God for the money He gives, but don't let money become your idol and steal your heart from God.

Help me to remember that money is Your gift to me, Lord. Examine my heart, show me where I am greedy, and help me to repent.

Week 47   Wednesday

HE'S ALL I NEED

The Lord is my shepherd; I shall not want.

Psalm 23:1

Shepherding is an ancient profession still practiced in cultures around the world. What's so important about sheep? More valuable than their wool or their meat are the lessons we can learn from them about our relationship with God.

Why does the Bible so often compare us to sheep? People are very much like sheep in several ways. Like sheep, people must be led. Like sheep, we tend to wander away from the fold. We are helpless in the face of predators, just like sheep. Sheep have trouble getting along with other sheep. Sound familiar? Most importantly, sheep are totally dependent on the shepherd. God is the shepherd; we are the sheep.

And so David writes, "The Lord is my shepherd; I shall not want." The Word of God is saying this: because the Lord is my shepherd, I have all I need. Because the Lord is my shepherd, I'll never lack for anything. Because the Lord is my shepherd, my life is not empty but full.

Jesus is our good shepherd. He has laid down His life for His sheep. Is the Lord your shepherd? Then you have all you need.

You are the shepherd, Lord, and I am Your sheep. Thank You that I want for nothing because You are all I need.

Week 47   Thursday

KNOCK

And I tell you, ask, and it will be given to you; seek, and you will find; knock, and it will be opened to you. For everyone who asks receives, and the one who seeks finds, and to the one who knocks it will be opened.

Luke 11:9-10

Every Tuesday, our church staff gathers to pray together over the prayer needs of our congregation. There are some people who submit the same requests every week, sometimes for years: "Pray for my husband and children to be saved." "Pray for my child to be delivered from drugs." "Pray for my mom with cancer."

Does God become weary of our same requests over and over? No. God's Word encourages us to never give up praying for these things. He encourages us to *knock, and keep on knocking.*

To *knock* means to pray with endurance. God is on the other side of the door. We are to knock until He opens the door.

The devil will whisper in your ear, "Why don't you quit? They're tired of hearing your need. And you're tired of not having an answer. God's forgotten you. Just quit."

Don't ever give up knocking on God's door. Keep knocking in prayer until you receive His answer. Keep on praying. You do not know when He will answer or how, but to the one who knocks, *it will be opened.*

Father, you are on the other side of the door, and You hear me knocking. Thank You for promising to open the door. Help me to be patient and wait for You.

Week 47   Friday

SEEK

And I tell you, ask, and it will be given to you; seek, and you will find; knock, and it will be opened to you. For everyone who asks receives, and the one who seeks finds, and to the one who knocks it will be opened.

Luke 11:9-10

One day, when our son, Joshua, was little, he spied an action figure he wanted at the toy store and asked me for it. I couldn't get it that day, but I said next time we were there, I would buy it for him. On our next visit to the store, the toy was gone. Joshua asked, "Daddy, do you promise you'll get that for me if we find it?" I promised him I would.

From that day on, he looked for that toy. In every store we visited he scoured the toy aisles for that one thing. He put a lot of effort and hundreds of steps into getting the toy he wanted. Joshua was seeking that toy.

To "seek" means to put effort and obedience behind your prayers. If you are seeking the Lord for an A on an exam, then studying would be your effort and obedience behind your prayer. If you are seeking God's blessing on your family, your effort and obedience would be to lead them spiritually. Unless we are obeying, then we're not really seeking.

Don't let a lack of effort or disobedience be the cause of God saying "no" when you seek Him.

Father, help me to obey all You show me when I seek Your answer to my prayers.

Week 48 — Monday

THE NARROW WAY

For this is the will of God, your sanctification: that you abstain from sexual immorality; that each one of you know how to control his own body in holiness and honor, not in the passion of lust like the Gentiles who do not know God;

1 Thessalonians 4:3-5

Do you remember the tumultuous '60s? Vietnam, assassinations, civil unrest, and drugs topped the news every evening. And leading the culture shift of the '60s was the sexual revolution. We'd never seen anything like it. Or had we?

Sex the world's way has been part of the human experience since sin entered the world. Amazingly, if you read the Bible from Genesis to Revelation, you'll find that throughout the ages, even among God's chosen people, sexual sin and perversion appear as much or even more than other types of sin.

Does that mean sex is bad? No! Sex is the wonderful creation of God. Sex is given by God not only for the creation of life, but for enjoyment and intimacy, but only under one condition: in marriage between a man and a woman. That's it. Sex under any other condition is sin.

In our "anything goes" world of sexual perversion, does that sound narrow to you? It is narrow. But God's command concerning our purity and holiness is for both His glory and our protection. God will not bless sex any other way.

Lord, I repent of all sexual sin, both of my body and of my mind. By the Holy Spirit's power, help me to control my thoughts and my body to bring You glory.

Week 48   Tuesday

GOD'S IN THE RESTORATION BUSINESS

Jesus stood up and said to her, "Woman, where are they? Has no one condemned you? She said, "No one, Lord." And Jesus said, "Neither do I condemn you; go, and from now on sin no more."

John 8:10

Many antique lovers are in the restoration business, scouring estate sales and dusty attics for valuable items that may appear hardly worth salvaging. But to the educated antique lover, they are pieces that with love and care can be restored to their original state, without blemish.

If you are engaged in a sexually sinful lifestyle now, or have been in the past, God offers hope for you. He loves you with all of His heart. Jesus Christ died to pay the penalty for your sexual sin, and every other sin in your life. He can restore you to sexual purity.

The adulterous woman was thrown at Jesus' feet by those who zealously condemned her. In those days, she could have been stoned for her sin. However, Jesus offered forgiveness to her. But it's so important to note the last thing He said to her: "From now on, sin no more."

God can restore you to sexual purity when you forsake your sin and seek Him with all your heart. Through Jesus Christ, you can experience total forgiveness of sin and a brand new start. Remember, Jesus came not to condemn you, but to save (John 3:17). To Him, you are worth it.

Lord Jesus, thank You that Your blood cleanses me completely from all my sin. I repent of my sexual sin, and ask that You would restore me to purity in Your eyes.

Week 48   Wednesday

A Living Link

After this the Lord appointed seventy-two others and sent them on ahead of Him, two by two, into every town and place where He Himself was about to go.

Luke 10:1

In 1930, King George V of England was scheduled to deliver a very important speech, broadcast by radio to millions of people, both in England and the United States. Just before he began to speak, at one of the radio stations, someone tripped over a wire and disconnected the transmitter. Instantly, the message was unavailable to the millions of people listening.

A young engineer at the station picked up both ends of the live wires and held them together. Electricity coursed through his body as he held the wires together. His body shook and trembled, but for twenty minutes he held on to the connection so people could hear the king's speech. He became a living connection between the king and the people.

Jesus sent the seventy-two to be a link between their world and Jesus. God has called you to be a living link between King Jesus and people in your world who need to hear about Him.

We are part of a holy triangle. God desires to save people. Searching souls need to hear the gospel of Jesus Christ. We are the living link that God uses to deliver His message. Will you bring the King's message to someone today?

Father, help me to be the link between the Lord Jesus and someone who needs to hear the gospel today.

Week 48   Thursday

NO BETTER, NO WORSE

My brothers, show no partiality as you hold the faith in our Lord Jesus Christ, the Lord of glory.

James 2:1

Modern skyscrapers are awe inspiring. But when they fall, they are all reduced to big piles of their contents: steel, glass, and concrete – the same common materials used to construct lesser buildings: hospitals, shopping malls, schools, and prisons.

Some structures may appear less dignified than others, but the purpose and design of each is decided by the architect. When they are demolished, every pile of contents will look the same. The pile may be steeper for some than others, but all contain the same stuff: steel and concrete and glass.

Partiality goes by many names, among them prejudice, favoritism, bigotry, chauvinism. No matter what we call it, God says, "Don't show partiality!" God is the architect of every life. Regardless of appearance, you are not better, nor are you inferior to anyone because of your differences.

Ask God to give you His heart of love for every person He allows across your path. Be ready to share the gospel with everyone. Welcome every person into the body of Christ without partiality. And allow God to demolish the sin of partiality in your life.

O God, help me to never be partial in favor of or against any person because of who they are or what they have. Help me to love every person like You love every person.

239

Week 48

Friday

Two Sides of the Same Coin

What good is it, my brothers, if someone says he has faith but does not have works? Can that faith save him? If a brother or sister is poorly clothed and lacking in daily food, and one of you says to them, "Go in peace, be warmed and filled," without giving them the things needed for the body, what good is that? So also faith by itself, if it does not have works, is dead.

James 2:14-17

When you're hungry, you might pop in a few quarters into a vending machine for a quick snack. The machine is smart enough to examine every coin. If the coins are good, then you get a snack. But if not, then no bag of chips for you! A coin not correctly minted on both sides is worthless.

Salvation is like a two-sided coin. When we have saving faith in Jesus Christ, God stamps the image of His Son on our hearts, like the image of George Washington is stamped on a quarter. You are now identified as belonging to Jesus. When God looks at you, He sees the righteousness of His Son.

God marks the other side of the coin as well. He has prepared good works for you to do in Jesus' name after you are saved. Those good works etch the proof of genuine faith on your life, and are visible to other people. In other words, when you get saved, you also get busy!

Genuine saving faith is not one-sided. Both faith in Jesus Christ and works of righteousness will be present in a person who is really saved. Faith without works is dead!

Lord, I can't work my way to a relationship with You. Thank You for saving me through the power of the gospel. Produce good works in my life as evidence of my salvation.

Week 49   Monday

PRICE IS NO OBJECT!

He who did not spare His own Son but gave Him up for us all,
how will He not also with Him graciously give us all things?
Romans 8:32

Let's say money is no object this holiday season. You open your computer, sit back and shop. There's the perfect gift for the girl living in Alaska: a Russian sable fur coat for only $74,500. Want to pop the question this Christmas? Grab a 4.5 carat diamond ring for $178,000. For the camera lover, there's a $26,000 zoom lens to slide into his stocking.

It's unthinkable for most of us to give such costly gifts. However, God spared no expense when He gave the gift of His Son, Jesus Christ, to us. God paid the highest price to purchase our redemption. The cost to set our souls free from the penalty of sin was unimaginable, except to God. "For God so loved the world that He gave His only begotten Son, that whosoever believes in Him should not perish but have everlasting life." (John 3:16).

Because God gave His Son, Jesus Christ, to pay the price for our sin, we can be sure that God loves us.

God. Loves. You. There is no question. He desires to give the gift of salvation to you, but you must accept it. Will you receive Jesus?

The very best gift ever given wasn't wrapped in paper and bows,
but in flesh. Thank You, God, for the gift of Jesus Christ!

Week 49 — Tuesday

WRONG NEST

And the Lord turned to him and said, "Go in this might of yours and save Israel from the hand of Midian; do not I send you?" And he said to Him, "Please, Lord, how can I save Israel? Behold, my clan is the weakest in Manasseh, and I am the least in my father's house." And the Lord said to him, "But I will be with you, and you shall strike the Midianites as one man."

Judges 6:14-16

A hunter found an eagle egg on the ground. He deposited it in a prairie chicken's nest, where it hatched after some time. The mother prairie chicken noticed the young bird was different, but guarded him as her own chick.

The eaglet was raised as a prairie chicken, pecking the ground for his food, thinking prairie chicken thoughts, never spreading his wings but living firmly attached to the ground. One day, he heard the call of a mighty eagle flying overhead. Raising his eyes Heavenward, he watched the eagle soar higher and higher until it disappeared. He thought, "I wish I could fly like that." Then he went back to pecking and scratching.

God saves us prairie chickens and makes us eagles! Yet, too many of us have been conditioned to believe that we are something significantly less than God has saved us to be. God called Gideon to a task too big for him. Gideon seriously doubted God, but God was faithful to Gideon and helped him to overwhelmingly complete his assignment. He will help you, too.

When God calls, He also enables. Faithful is He who calls you, and He will bring it to pass.

In Christ I have all the power I need to do Your will. On my own I am powerless, but because Your Holy Spirit lives in me, Lord, I can do anything You ask of me!

Week 49   Wednesday

RECEIVE THE SON

He is the image of the invisible God, the firstborn of all creation.
Colossians 1:15

A wealthy art collector lost his son in war. One day a soldier came to visit, and revealed that the son had been killed while rescuing him. The surviving soldier presented the grieving father a painting of his son. Though not expertly done, the father, deeply grateful, cleared a place over the mantel to display the prized image of his precious son.

At his death, the father's magnificent art collection was auctioned. As his will stipulated, the painting of his son was auctioned first. No one bid on the amateur work. Finally, the man's long-time housekeeper, who had loved the boy, bid $50 on the painting. No one challenged. The gavel fell, and the auctioneer cried, "Sold! The auction is complete." The collectors were flabbergasted and insisted the auction continue. "The will is clear," replied the auctioneer. "Whoever takes the son receives everything."

That's the message of Christmas. When you take the Son, you get everything else the Father has. Jesus Christ, the baby in the manger, is the image of the one true God. Your Christmas can be one of joy when you remember that when God gave Jesus, He gave us all of Himself. What an awesome gift!

When I look at You, Jesus, I see the Father. You are God in the flesh. Thank You for coming to us!

Week 49   Thursday

THE CHRISTMAS MIRACLE

Seek the Lord and His strength; seek His presence continually! Remember the wondrous works that He has done, His miracles, and the judgments He uttered, O offspring of Abraham, His servant, children of Jacob, His chosen ones!

Psalm 105:4-6

Did you know there's a whole list of Christmas "miracle" movies? "Miracle on 34th Street," "The Christmas Miracle," "A Season for Miracles," "Holiday Miracle," "Mrs. Miracle." It seems that the world has a market on "miracles" during the Christmas season.

Here's a short list of real miracles: A virgin conceived and gave birth to the Son of God. The eternal Son of God became a man. Jesus was tempted in every way as we are, yet never sinned. Jesus was innocent of any sin, yet willingly laid His body on a cross to die for the sins of mankind. He rose from the grave on the third day. He ascended to the right hand of the Father, where He ever lives to make intercession for us. He gives eternal life to everyone who calls on His name. He is coming again to receive us to Himself, that where He is, there we may be also.

Through faith in Jesus Christ, we experience His miracle of redemption and restoration to God, and the power of the indwelling Holy Spirit every moment of every day. Don't confine your expectation of miracles to Christmas. In Christ, our entire life is a season of miracles!

O Father, You are truly the God of miracles! Thank You for the miracle You did in my life when You saved me and gave me new life in Christ!

244

Week 49 — Friday

THE GOSPEL FOR CHRISTMAS

When they saw the star, they rejoiced exceedingly with great joy. And going into the house they saw the Child with Mary His mother, and they fell down and worshiped Him. Then, opening their treasures, they offered Him gifts, gold and frankincense and myrrh.

Matthew 2:10-11

Christmas is a time for decisions. Artificial tree or real? Turkey or ham? Stay home or travel? Pecan or pumpkin pie? Dinner with your family or his? But perhaps the biggest decision we must make is this: what kind of heart will I have for Christmas?

Will you rejoice as Christmas approaches, or will you be complacent? The real magnificence of Christmas is only truly visible through the gospel of Jesus Christ. Remember, without the virgin birth, there would be no acceptable sacrifice for sin. Without sacrifice for sin, there would be no forgiveness. Without forgiveness, there can be no eternal life. Without eternal life, there can be no joy! Without Christmas there is no gospel, and without the gospel, there can be no joyful Christmas.

This year, I hope you will choose a heart of joy for Christmas. The trappings of a materialistic Christmas will leave you wanting, every time. But when we dwell on the good news of the gospel, only made possible by the birth of God's Son, we find great reason to rejoice. This year, enjoy the gospel for Christmas!

Lord, I know that real joy for Christmas is my choice. Today, I choose to spend Christmas rejoicing in Jesus!

Week 50   Monday

Perfect Peace

You keep him in perfect peace whose mind is stayed on You, because he trusts in You.

Isaiah 26:3

You have probably seen a variety show or circus act where someone spins plates on wooden dowels. As frenetic music plays in the background, the performer attempts to have as many plates as possible spinning at once. One man in Thailand actually managed to keep 108 plates spinning simultaneously.

Do you ever feel like your life is becoming a plate-spinning act? There may be days when it seems like you have to do everything, say everything, go everywhere, and be everything all at once. Thankfully, God is able to deliver you from the tyranny of a frantic life. When your life becomes overwhelmingly hectic and your mind becomes tangled up with worries, God offers peace.

In the Hebrew language, God's beautiful word for peace is shalom. The words of Isaiah 26:3 translated "perfect peace" are actually "shalom shalom." To show the completeness and perfection of the peace God gives, the word is doubled. When your cares are multiplied, so is God's peace! When everything happens all at once, trust in Him. Turn your thoughts toward the Lord, His power, His grace, His mercy, and His goodness. He will give you complete peace.

Take a moment to trust God for all the demands of your day.

Thank you, Father, that in You I can have peace. Give me grace to trust You when my life becomes hectic and difficult.

Week 50   *Tuesday*

NEW GLASSES FOR CHRISTMAS

I do not cease to give thanks for you, remembering you in my prayers, that the God of our Lord Jesus Christ, the Father of glory, may give you the Spirit of wisdom and of revelation in the knowledge of Him.

Ephesians 1:16-17

Often, children do poorly in school until the teacher or parents perceive that the problem is not lack of understanding but that the child cannot see the board. Once fitted with glasses, a child's life in the classroom changes drastically.

The lens that will correct our vision of Christmas is God's Word. The world tells us Christmas is about gifts; the Bible tells us Christmas is about THE gift. The world says Christmas is about parties; the Bible tells us Christmas is about a heavenly celebration. The world says Christmas is about a sweet little baby in a manger; the Bible tells us that Christmas is about the birth of the King of kings and Lord of lords. For the world, Christmas stops at 11:59 p.m. on December 25. But the Bible tells us that the story of Christmas has its completion 33 years after the shepherds came running to Bethlehem, when the sinless Son of God rose from the grave after paying for the sins of mankind!

Christmas is so much more than the world tells us. This Christmas, look at Christmas through the lens of scripture. You may just see things you've never seen before!

Clear up my vision of Christmas this year, Lord, so that I can see Your glory and find joy in the true meaning of Christmas.

Week 50   Wednesday

WE NEED A SILENT NIGHT

And in the same region there were shepherds out in the field, keeping watch over their flock by night. And an angel of the Lord appeared to them, and the glory of the Lord shone around them, and they were filled with great fear. And the angel said to them, "Fear not, for behold, I bring you good news of great joy that will be for all the people. For unto you is born this day in the city of David a Savior, who is Christ the Lord."

Luke 2:8-11

"Silent Night" is the world's favorite Christmas carol. But silence can be pretty hard to come by during the season. I imagine that hanging out with a crew of sleepy shepherds and a flock of bleating sheep might offer the only quiet to be found while our list of seasonal demands screams at us.

You might even make a list of things you want to do for yourself when you finally get a little quiet during the Christmas rush. However, the greatest benefit to us when we finally have a silent moment at Christmas comes from resting in Jesus and meditating on the meaning of the baby in the manger.

We often completely bypass the peace that Jesus brought with His birth. We sing about it, we even display figures that tell the story. But we never sit still long enough to let it sink in.

Is peace at Christmas unable to take root in your heart because of the rocky soil of holiday busyness? In the silence, the story of Christmas still speaks the best news of all: "Unto you is born this day in the City of David a Savior, who is Christ the Lord!"

My schedule of events and chores for Christmas is long. Lord, help me to schedule time for quiet with You so I can meditate on the wonderful news that Jesus Christ was born for me.

Week 50   Thursday

WHAT DO YOU WANT FOR CHRISTMAS?

When they saw the star, they rejoiced exceedingly with great joy. And going into the house they saw the Child with Mary His mother, and they fell down and worshiped Him. Then, opening their treasures, they offered Him gifts, gold and frankincense and myrrh.

Matthew 2:10-11

Every year at Christmas time, marketers tell us what we want for Christmas. Cheery Christmas tunes play while desirable items are paraded before us. Who wouldn't want a beautiful car tied with a bow so large it wouldn't fit in the garage, or latest greatest electronic device that will "do it all?"

But think about the things you want all year: You want your kids to do well. You want freedom from an addiction. You want the money needed to pay your bills. You want peace when a loved one has left you. You want wisdom when you don't know which way to turn. And you want life when confronted by illness and death. These are gifts that cannot be wrapped with shiny paper and big bows.

What we all really want really boils down to one thing: we want real peace that passes understanding in the face of really hard, life altering circumstances. The world cannot give it to you, but Jesus can.

The wise men brought fine gifts to Jesus, but He gave greater gifts to them, and to all who would believe in His name. He gives life and real peace to all who call on His name.

Thank You for Your gift of peace, Jesus. I've tried finding it in other things, but real peace only comes from You. I ask You for it as I celebrate Christmas.

Week 50

TOMATOES AND FRUIT SALAD

For whoever finds me finds life and obtains favor from the LORD, but he who fails to find me injures himself; all who hate me love death.
                                                            Proverbs 8:35–36

Michele and I once saw a greeting card with these words: "Knowledge is knowing that a tomato is a fruit. Wisdom is not putting it in a fruit salad." I couldn't help from laughing! Wisdom really is more than just the accumulation of information. Wisdom always proves itself in what we do. In spiritual terms, wisdom means understanding life from God's perspective and then living accordingly.

God's Word has much to say about wisdom. Proverbs 3:19 tells us God created the universe through wisdom and understanding. Psalm 104:24 says all living creatures, including mankind, were made by God's wisdom. Psalm 111:10 is one of several places in Scripture that reminds us the fear of the Lord is the beginning of wisdom.

In Proverbs 8, wise King Solomon wrote about wisdom's powers and virtues. He concluded by saying that whoever finds wisdom finds life and God's favor, but whoever rejects wisdom finds injury and death. We receive wisdom from the hand of God, in the Word of God, by the fear of God, and, most fully, in the Son of God. When we come to Jesus, His atoning work on the cross is the wisdom of God for salvation.

I praise You, Lord, for giving me wisdom when I ask. Guide my steps by Your wisdom as I seek to follow Jesus throughout my day.

Week 51   Monday

TODAY'S HEADLINE

...the time is fulfilled, and the kingdom of God is at hand; repent and believe in the gospel.

Mark 1:15

Here's a wonderful Christmas meditation written by my friend, Kim Jackson:

It's Christmas time, a time for family, gifts, and special events. We enjoy beautiful imagery, glorious music, and wonderful food. But Christmas bears history's greatest headline: Jesus Came! The Bible answers all six important investigative questions about Jesus.

Who was He? He was God's Son: "And the Word became flesh and dwelt among us, and we have seen His glory, glory as of the only Son from the Father, full of grace and truth." (John 1:14)

What did He do? "He was pierced for our transgressions; He was crushed for our iniquities; upon Him was the chastisement that brought us peace, and with His wounds we are healed." (Isaiah 53:5)

When did He do it? "But when the fullness of time had come, God sent forth His Son, born of a virgin, born under the law." (Galatians 4:4)

Where? "'And you, O Bethlehem, in the land of Judah, are by no means least among the rulers of Judah; for from you shall come a ruler who will shepherd my people Israel.'" (Matthew 2:6)

Why did He do it? "For God so loved the world, that He gave His only Son, that whoever believes in Him should not perish but have eternal life." (John 3:16)

How did He do it? "Christ died for our sins in accordance with the Scriptures, that He was buried, that He was raised on

the third day in accordance with the Scriptures."
(1 Corinthians 15:3-4)

The only question the Bible doesn't answer is this: How will you respond to the story of Jesus? Will you throw it aside, like yesterday's newspaper? Perhaps you're intrigued by the story, but are withholding your commitment to it because you don't really think you need it.

But if you will receive it by faith, if you will repent of your sin and personally trust Jesus Christ as Savior and Lord, He will forgive all of your sin and give you the gift of eternal life. Then you will have a great personal story to share.

Jesus Christ came to save sinners. It's the greatest story ever told.

Lord Jesus, Your story truly is the greatest story ever told. Your story is not just another Christmas tale; Your story is true. Thank You for coming to save the world. Thank You for coming to save me! Help me worship You in every celebration of Christmas.

For more information about trusting Jesus Christ, turn to page 263.

Week 51   Tuesday

THE BIRTH ANNOUNCEMENT

She will bear a Son, and you shall call His name Jesus, for He will save His people from their sins." All this took place to fulfill what the Lord had spoken by the prophet: "Behold, the virgin shall conceive and bear a Son, and they shall call His name Immanuel."

Matthew 1:21-23

He who testifies to these things says, "Surely I am coming soon. Amen. Come, Lord Jesus!"

Revelation 22:20

Birth announcements are a wonderful way for parents to share the arrival of precious children. But it would be very unusual to send a birth announcement before the baby is born.

However, seven hundred years before the birth of Christ, God revealed, through the prophet Isaiah, that a virgin would give birth to a son. Isaiah even announced one of His names – Immanuel, which means "God with us." God announced to Israel that He was coming to visit them. That was exciting news!

Yet, as time and hardship took their toll, many Israelites lost sight of God's promised coming. But at the right time and in exactly the manner God promised, Immanuel did come. He came not only for the Jews who were living at the time He was born, but He also came for you and me.

Another announcement has been made: Jesus is coming again! Are you looking forward to that day? Don't lose hope when life is hard. At just the right time, and in just the way God has promised, Jesus will return for us. Today, you can have joy because Jesus is coming again.

Lord Jesus, I am so grateful You came the first time to die for me. I look forward to Your return so I can be with You!

Week 51   Wednesday

HEAVEN'S PERSPECTIVE

And the angel said to them, "Fear not, for behold, I bring you good news of great joy that will be for all the people. For unto you is born this day in the city of David a Savior, who is Christ the Lord. And this will be a sign for you: you will find a Baby wrapped in swaddling cloths and lying in a manger." And suddenly there was with the angel a multitude of the heavenly host praising God and saying, "Glory to God in the highest, and on earth peace among those with whom He is pleased!"

Luke 2:10-14

It would seem that a poor couple lodged in a dirty stable in an unfriendly town, bringing a baby into a world surrounded by animals and forced to use a feed trough for a bed would have little reason for celebration. Yet, Mary and Joseph probably celebrated Christmas better than anyone else ever has.

This young couple was given a vision of God's purpose and was personally involved in the fulfillment of His centuries-old promise. They understood their desperate need for a Savior, and they were awestruck to have been chosen by God to be part of His plan.

Mary and Joseph's lives were interrupted by angels, shepherds, and kings. Are you willing to be interrupted by God so He can work His purpose through you? Are you willing to be involved in the continuing story of Christmas? God's gift of His Son is as much for us as it was for Mary and Joseph.

God has promised that all who come to His Son in repentance and faith will be saved from their sin, have their fears allayed and their needs met, and will be with Him forever. Having that perspective on Christmas will help us have a true celebration!

The Christmas story is two thousand years old, and yet it is for me! Thank You, Lord, that it brings me salvation.

254

Week 51 — Thursday

THE BEST GIFT OF ALL

And You, Child, will be called the prophet of the Most High; for You will go before the Lord to prepare His ways, to give knowledge of salvation to His people in the forgiveness of their sins, because of the tender mercy of our God, whereby the sunrise shall visit us from on high to give light to those who sit in darkness and in the shadow of death, to guide our feet into the way of peace.

Luke 1:76-79

When Michele and I shopped for Christmas gifts for Joshua as he was growing up, we usually got him something that would make him really happy, but we also got him something he really needed. A teenage boy might not be ecstatic over all new socks for Christmas, but if we wrapped up a new electronic device, you could pretty much guarantee he'd be happy on Christmas day.

The gift of God's Son meets all gift giving criteria: it meets our deepest need, the forgiveness of our sin, and it brings unspeakable joy. In Christ, God gave us light to lead us from darkness and the shadow of death, and to guide us in the way of peace.

As you give and receive gifts this year, remember God's gift to you of His Son. He paid the absolute highest price to present us the very greatest gift: the life of His Son to purchase our salvation. It's also a gift you can share with someone who hasn't yet received it. Who can you share Jesus with this Christmas?

There is no other gift that compares to the gift of Jesus. Thank You, Father, that Your gift of Your Son is for me personally. Help me share it with someone today.

Week 51

WHEN THREAD WON'T DO

And without faith it is impossible to please Him, for whoever would draw near to God must believe that He exists and that He rewards those who seek Him.

Hebrews 11:6

Dr. D. James Kennedy, founder of Evangelism Explosion International, once asked his readers to imagine trying to cross a deep, rocky canyon, 100 feet wide. You have a thick, sturdy rope in hand, but it is only 50 feet long. What if someone offered 50 feet of slender thread, saying, "Tie your rope to this, it will stretch across the whole chasm?" You would refuse because the thread would never hold you up.

Then Dr. Kennedy changed the story, first making the rope 90 feet long and the thread 10 feet long, and then making the rope 99 feet and 11 inches long, with only one inch of thread. Still, you would never try to cross. He concluded, "If you have one inch of thread, you will be just as dead on the rocks below as if you try to cross on a hundred feet of thread."

His point was the hopelessness of placing faith in anything or anyone other than Jesus. Faith means trusting that God is who He says He is and that He will do what He has promised to do. By faith, we know God that offers salvation, a glorious future, and strength for each day to everyone who follows Jesus.

Dear Lord Jesus, I believe that You provide everything I need for now and for eternity. Give me Your grace to trust You for each moment of my life.

Week 52   Monday

A WELL DESIGNED TRAP

Let no one say when he is tempted, "I am being tempted by God," for God cannot be tempted with evil, and he himself tempts no one. But each person is tempted when he is lured and enticed by his own desire.

James 1:13-14

Charlotte's Web is the moving story of a very smart spider that helps save the life of a little girl's pig. The story has a great ending ... for *almost* everyone. Insects lured into Charlotte's trap suffer a tragic ending.

Like Charlotte's web, temptation is very enticing. But when we hang around too close to it and fail to understand the strategy of our enemy, we fall into sin, and it is deadly.

God's Word clearly teaches us how to recognize temptation and gives specific steps to deal with it so we can avoid becoming tangled up in it. Be assured that God will never tempt you. He is holy; He cannot be tempted, nor will He tempt anyone. Temptation will come from either the devil or from our own desires. We need to train ourselves to recognize it and then take every step to escape it before we become trapped in sin.

What are you tempted by today? God is faithful and will strengthen you and provide a way of escape. You can be victorious over sin! When tempted, look for God's way of escape, and remind the devil you're taking it. Don't hang around the trap of sin.

I'm tempted every day by something, and sometimes it seems so small. Lord Jesus, help me to run from temptation before small things become big in my life.

Week 52   Tuesday

DISCOURAGED?

Be strong and let your heart take courage, all you who wait for the LORD.

Psalm 31:24

In 1836, architect Robert Mills was thrilled that the Washington National Monument Society had chosen his plans for a monument to the nation's first president. His grand vision of building the 555 foot obelisk seemed to take off. But then...

Funding dried up; construction was delayed for a total of twelve years. The ground at the site proved too soft, requiring relocation. Vandals defaced the construction. The project was halted in 1855. A year later, Robert Mills died, having only experienced discouragement.

When you're discouraged, don't let your emotions fool you. They may tell you you're no good, you can't win, that you have no friends, it will never get better, and you might as well give up. Sound familiar?

A discouraged heart can lead you away from God. Listen to what God says about you. He loves you with an everlasting love. Jesus loves you enough to die for you. He has a hope and a future for you. He wants the best for your life. He is working all things, even the discouraging things, together for your good.

Don't allow your emotions to mislead you when discouraged. Instead, go to God's Word and be encouraged by His love and His heart toward you.

Some days are discouraging, Lord. Help me to continually look to You, Lord, to hear the truth about me from Your perspective.

Week 52 — Wednesday

THE REMEDY FOR DISCOURAGEMENT

There he came to a cave and lodged in it. And behold, the word of the Lord came to him, and He said to him, "What are you doing here, Elijah?" He said, "I have been very jealous for the Lord, the God of hosts. For the people of Israel have forsaken your covenant, thrown down your altars, and killed your prophets with the sword, and I, even I only, am left, and they seek my life, to take it away."

1 Kings 19:9-10

I've never met anyone who has not experienced times of discouragement in their life. Perhaps you're experiencing discouragement right now. When circumstances are difficult, you're not making progress in life, or you're feeling devalued, discouragement can creep in. Discouragement is not a sin. But it can open the door to temptation and lead to a number of sins.

Elijah had been faithful to the Lord. He had been used mightily by God to defeat the prophets of Baal and to withstand the evil King Ahab and Queen Jezebel. Yet, after all that, Elijah went away by himself, feeling abandoned, alone, defeated, and discouraged. He wanted to die, and even asked God to take his life.

God's response to Elijah was to let him rest, provide food for him to eat, and to speak to him to encourage him. He made Himself known to Elijah, and Elijah was strengthened.

Discouragement can cause us to make rash or unwise decisions. When you are discouraged, ask God to take defeat and discouragement out of your spirit. Take some time to rest. Have something good to eat. Let God's Word speak to you. God wants to refresh and encourage you.

Lord, encourage me by Your Word, and make me an encouragement to someone who needs refreshing today.

Week 52   *Thursday*

DISCOURAGEMENT AND BAMBOO TREES

David also said to Solomon his son, "Be strong and courageous, and do the work. Do not be afraid or discouraged, for the Lord God, my God, is with you. He will not fail you or forsake you until all the work for the service of the temple of the Lord is finished.

1 Chronicles 28:20

God has made everything for a purpose. Sometimes, His creation helps us understand lessons about life. Take the bamboo tree, for example. That particular plant does nothing, it would seem, for the first four years of its life. Then suddenly, sometime during its fifth year, it shoots up ninety feet in sixty days. Would you say the bamboo tree grew in six weeks, or five years?

Dave and Diana were called by God to take the gospel to a primitive tribe in Brazil. They excitedly went to work. For twenty years, they sowed, planted, and watered, but not one person in their tribe was saved. Many times, they were overcome with discouragement and questioned God's plan.

In year twenty-one, the first person of that tribe came to Christ. The harvest became so plentiful, that now, missionaries are being sent from that tribe to other tribes to share the gospel. Do you think the results came in 1 year, or in twenty-one years?

Do not let discouragement persuade you to abandon God's clear plan for your life. He will faithfully bring his desired results at the right time, and strengthen you to complete what He has called you to.

Lord, help me when I'm discouraged to remember that the plans are Yours, the timing is Yours, and the results are Yours. Help me to obey You with joy in my heart.

Week 52

Friday

Plastic Jesus

He said to them, "But who do you say that I am?" Simon Peter replied, "You are the Christ, the Son of the living God."
Matthew 16:15-16

A few years ago, a toy company sold a plastic Jesus doll. At the push of a button, he would say a verse of Scripture. If you had a Jesus doll, you could make him go where you wanted him to go, make him do what you want him to do, and say what you want him to say.

Many people have a plastic Jesus, in their own image, which says what they want to hear him say and doesn't say what they don't want to hear him say. Their plastic Jesus suits their own needs. He never offends, never challenges, never convicts, and never brings conflict into our lives.

The real Jesus is found in the Bible, from Genesis to Revelation. He will ask difficult things of us. He calls us to become like Him, not the other way around.

If you are following a plastic Jesus, then you are not following the Jesus of Scripture. If your Jesus is plastic, so are your hope and your salvation. Don't settle for an imitation Jesus. Only the real Jesus can save your soul.

Father, would You please show me where I've bought into the world's idea of who Jesus is? Help me to follow You as You are revealed in Scripture. Lord, You are the only true Jesus.

262

HOW TO BE SAVED

God says, "For 'everyone who calls on the name of the Lord will be saved.' " (Romans 10:13) This involves understanding and believing several things.

1. **Sin separates us from God.** "All have sinned and fall short of the glory of God." (Romans 3:23) Sin is anything about us that displeases God. We may sin in the things we say, in the things we do, or even in the things we think. Every person has sinned, and deserves eternal separation from God in Hell because of sin. "The wages of sin is death, but the gift of God is eternal life in Christ Jesus our Lord." (Romans 6:23)

2. **Jesus paid the price for our sin.** "God so loved the world that He gave His only begotten Son, that whoever believes in Him should not perish but have everlasting life." (John 3:16) Jesus - God's eternal Son - never sinned. When Jesus was crucified on the cross, He died in our place for our sins. God sent Jesus to die for us because He loves us. "God demonstrates His own love toward us, in that while we were still sinners, Christ died for us." (Romans 5:8)

3. **Salvation in found in Jesus alone.** "By grace you have been saved through faith, and that not of yourselves; it is the gift of God, not of works, lest anyone should boast." (Ephesians 2:8-9) Our goodness, morality, or religious activity will not make us right with God. Only by faith in Jesus Christ can a person be saved. "Nor is there salvation in any other, for there is no other name under Heaven given among men by which we must be saved" (Acts 4:12)

4. **We must trust Jesus personally.** In order to receive the gift of salvation, we must call on Christ. It's not enough just to know the truth about who Jesus is and what He did on the cross. Salvation requires turning from sin and asking the Lord to save us. "If you confess with your mouth the Lord Jesus and believe in your heart that God has raised Him from the dead, you will be saved." (Romans 10:9).

God's desire for you is to have eternal life with Him through His Son. If you would like to have a relationship with Jesus Christ, you can call on the Lord right now by simply praying a prayer like this:

"Lord Jesus, I know I am a sinner. I believe You died for my sins. Right now, I turn from my sins and ask for Your salvation. I trust You as my Lord and Savior. Thank You for saving me. Amen."

If you have prayed that prayer and meant it in your heart, Jesus Christ has saved you. Remember God's promise: *For "everyone who calls on the name of the Lord will be saved."*

We would love to rejoice with you! Please email info@stephenrummage.com and let us know you've prayed to receive Jesus Christ as Savior. We want to encourage you and get materials to you to help you in your new life in Jesus Christ.

Notes and Prayer Requests

Notes and Prayer Requests

Notes and Prayer Requests

Notes and Prayer Requests

Notes and Prayer Requests

Notes and Prayer Requests

Notes and Prayer Requests

Notes and Prayer Requests

Notes and Prayer Requests

Notes and Prayer Requests

Notes and Prayer Requests

Notes and Prayer Requests

Notes and Prayer Requests

Notes and Prayer Requests

Notes and Prayer Requests

Notes and Prayer Requests

Notes and Prayer Requests

Notes and Prayer Requests

NOTES

[1] Nancy Spiegelberg, "If Only I Had Known," (n.d.),
<http://www.godthoughts.com/known.html>. (Accessed 07-23-2015).

[2] Bronnie Ware, Hospice Patients Alliance, (n.d.),
<http://hospicepatients.org/five-regrets-of-the-dying-bronnie-ware.html>. (Accessed August 26, 2015).

[3] James Owen, "Tsunami Family Saved by Schoolgirl's Geography Lesson,"
January 18, 2005,
<http://news.nationalgeographic.com/news/2005/01/0118_050118_tsunami_geography_lesson.html>, National Geographic Society,
(Accessed July 21, 2015).

[4] Ravi Zacharias, <u>The Grand Weaver</u>. Grand Rapids, MI: Zondervan.
2007.

SCRIPTURAL INDEX

OLD TESTAMENT

GENESIS
2:22-24 83
4:7 179
22:12-14 217
37:8 213

DEUTERONOMY
6:4 146
6:5-7 148

JOSHUA
1:8 188
24:15 118

JUDGES
6:14-16 242

1 KINGS
19:9-10 260

1 CHRONICLES
16:11-13 48
28:20 261

PSALMS
1:1-2 ....116, 147
19:1–3 189
23:1 233
29:2 40
30:10-12 207
31:24 259
32:5 205
33:13-15 257
40:3 89
46:1-2 126
51:1-2 77
63:1 216
69:13 185

78:1 13
92:1-2 69
103:14 199
105:4-6 244
107:9 46
119:18 154
119:71 160
119:92-93 174
121:3-5 117
139:1-2 196

PROVERBS
1:5 45
4:20-22 214
8:35-36 250
16:9 162
19:5 150
22:1 208

ECCLESIASTES
3:1 39

ISAIAH
26:3 246
41:10 231
43:1-2 47
49:15 38
55:2-3 152

JEREMIAH
10:23 176
29:11 ....52, 193
31:34 169

EZEKIEL
36:25-27 108

JOEL
2:13 191

MICAH
7:18 41

ZECHARIAH
1:1-3 194
1:3.................................201
4:6.................................133

MALACHI
3:8-10...........................129
4:5-6.............................164

NEW TESTAMENT

MATTHEW
1:18-21 246
1:21-23 254
1:23...............................222
2:10-11 ....245, 250
4:19...............................161
4:21-22 153
5:2-3............................. 34
5:43-44 114
6:13...............................218
6:19-21 92
6:25-26 95
6:34..................................3
7:1-5.............................102
7:7-8.............................106
7:15...............................101
9:5-7.............................166
10:28............................. 20
13:14-16...........................7
16:15-16........................262
19:6............................... 82
20:26-28.......................151
22:37-40.......................107
24:42.............................177
25:23.............................200
27:45–46 60
28:18-19.......................110

MARK
1:15...............................252
1:16-20 172
5:15...............................184
6:30-31 9

7:8 202
8:35................................. 16
8:36-37........................... 14
9:46-48........................... 19
10:20-22 21
11:22-24 24
12:29-31 25
13:35-36 28
16:5-6............................. 64
16:6................................. 65
16:15 178

LUKE
1:76-79..........................256
2:8-11.............................249
2:10-14..........................255
2:15-18..........................251
10:1................................238
10:8-9.............................230
11:9-10 ....228, 234, 235
12:32..............................132
16:10-11 49
22:45-46 187
23:33-34 57
23:39-43 58
23:46 62

JOHN
1:11-12 87
1:14................................182
3:16................................263
3:16-17........................... 56
8:10................................237
8:44................................136
10:10 219
10:27-29 2
13:15 93
13:34-35 88
14:27 165
17:3................................. 26
19:26-27 59
19:28–29........................ 61
19:30 30

ACTS

2:21	167, 264
4:12	263
5:27-29	125
10:38	55
20:24	145
21:13	183

ROMANS

1:21	210
3:23	263
5:8	263
6:4	6
6:12-13	221
6:23	263
8:28	104
8:32	241
8:38-39	163
10:9	263
10:13	11, 263
10:14-15	186
12:1-2	143
13:1-2	123
13:13-14	128
15:4	113

1 CORINTHIANS

3:10-11	130
3:12-15	204
6:9-11	141
6:18-20	227
10:12	122
10:13	17
11:24-26	215
12:12-13	10
12:27	91
15:1-4	192
15:12-14	63
15:57	155
15:58	37

2 CORINTHIANS

3:18	149
5:9-10	36

5:10	203
5:17	1, 120
5:19	66
8:2	197
12:9	18
12:10	112
13:5	190

GALATIANS

1:7-8	170
5:1	71, 127
5:22-23	44
6:1	33
6:7	50

EPHESIANS

1:16-17	248
2:8-9	68, 263
3:20-21	156
4:22-24	223
4:31	84
5:1	74
5:2	84
5:3	90
5:8	75
5:8-10	97
5:11-13	100
5:15-16	157
5:15-17	22
5:22-24	85
5:25-27	86
5:33	173
6:5-8	72, 79
6:9	73
6:10-13	98
6:11	135
6:12	134
6:16	103

PHILIPPIANS

1:9-11	226
2:3-4	181
2:12-13	171
3:7-8	144

3:12-14 131
3:13-14 111
4:11-13 ....8, 175
4:19 4

COLOSSIANS
1:13 70
1:15 243
1:15-18 105
2:13 94
3:8-9 206
3:12-13 31
3:16 76

1 THESSALONIANS
1:2-3 ....159, 168
1:9 211
4:1 229
4:3-5 236
5:4-5 12
5:16-17 142
5:16-18 67

1 TIMOTHY
6:10 232

2 TIMOTHY
1:7 78

HEBREWS
4:12 224
4:15 15
5:11-14 220
9:27 42
10:24-25 225
11:6 256
12:2 5
13:4 81
13:8 119

JAMES
1:2-3 27
1:4 29
1:5 137
1:12 138
1:12-13 139

1:13-14 ....32, 140, 258
1:15 35
2:1 239
2:14-17 240
4:13-16 99

1 PETER
1:3-4 53
1:3-5 51
1:6-7 54
1:8 43
1:15 74
1:15-16 158
2:12 180
2:17 124
5:8-9 23

2 PETER
1:3 195
3:9 121

1 JOHN
1:1-3 109
1:9 198
2:15-17 209

REVELATION
5:11-12 115
5:13 212
17:14 96
20:10 80
22:20 254

TOPICAL INDEX

Abundance................................. 219
Abundant Life......................... 219
Access to God......................... 106
Advice.......................................93
Ambition.................................. 181
Anxiety..2
Aspirations.............................. 149
Authority...........................124, 125
Authority of God...................... 119
Awesomeness........................... 212

Baptism..6
Be a Disciple............................ 178
Being Pardoned..........................41
Belief..24
Bible..........................76, 101, 247
Blame...32
Blessings................................. 116
Boldness.................................. 230
Boss.............................. 72, 73, 79
Bridges.......................................66

Change...........................184, 206
Character................................. 208
Children................................... 148
Choices.................................... 118
Christmas.........244, 245, 247, 248,
249,251, 253, 254, 255
Christmas Miracle.................... 244
Church Body...................91, 225
Clean..77
Comfort................................... 113
Comforter...................................15
Completion.................................30
Compounding Joy.................... 197
Connections............................. 238
Contentment...............................8
Crown of Life........................... 138
Crucifixion.................................61

Dad.. 74
Death... 54
Deception.........................136, 150
Decisions..................................245
Deliverance................................ 70
Desires......................................216
Disciples...................................178
Discouragement........98, 103, 141,
258, 259, 260

Emotions......................7, 155, 258
Employee................................... 72
Encouragement........................113
Encouraging Words..................141
End.. 80
Enemies....................................114
Enemy.......................................136
Examination.............................190
Examples................................... 93
Expectancy...............................228
Extremes...................................207

Failure......................................112
Faith...256
Faith in Jesus............................171
Faithfulness..............................172
Falsehood.................................101
Family.. 59
Father.. 74
Fear.............................20, 78, 231
Final Words............................... 62
Fishing for Souls.......................161
Focus...............................23, 131
Following Jesus...................21, 153
Forgetting.................................. 38
Forgiveness............31, 84, 94, 174
Forgiving..................................169
Foundations...................130, 204

Freedom	127	Guilt	198, 205
Fundamentals	192		
		Happiness	44
Gifts	249, 255	Harvest	50
Goals	131	Heaven	195, 254
God's Abundance	4	Hell	19
God's Anger	194	Holy Spirit	133
God's Authority	125	Holy Triangle	238
God's Calling	242	Honoring	124
God's Design	193	Honoring Jesus	108
God's Direction	162, 176	Hope	52, 168, 213
God's Discipline	160	Hope in Jesus	65
God's Forgiveness	57, 169	Hopelessness	256
God's Gift	241	Husband	85
God's Glory	180	Husbands	173

Freedom 127
Fundamentals 192

Gifts 249, 255
Goals 131
God's Abundance 4
God's Anger 194
God's Authority 125
God's Calling 242
God's Design 193
God's Direction 162, 176
God's Discipline 160
God's Forgiveness 57, 169
God's Gift 241
God's Glory 180
God's Greatness 189
God's Holy Spirit 227
God's Humility 181
God's Love 14
God's Majesty 212
God's Mercy 194
God's Patience 121
God's Plan 176
God's Power 218
God's Promises 58, 78,
                   103, 175, 254
God's Protection 126
God's Righteousness 221
God's Son 255
God's Spirit 199
God's Standard 158
God's Voice 227
God's Warnings 179
God's Wealth 132
God's Will 143, 209
God's Wisdom 137
God's Word 188, 224, 257
Good Death 62
Good Shepherd 233
Gospel 102, 251
Greed 232
Grieving 207
Growing 184

Guilt 198, 205

Happiness 44
Harvest 50
Heaven 195, 254
Hell 19
Holy Spirit 133
Holy Triangle 238
Honoring 124
Honoring Jesus 108
Hope 52, 168, 213
Hope in Jesus 65
Hopelessness 256
Husband 85
Husbands 173

Idols 211
Intimacy 81

Jehovah Jireh 217
Jesus the Son 243
Jesus' Birth 253
Jesus' Body 91
Jesus' Cleansing 202
Jesus' Love 107, 114
Jesus' Perfect Life 222
Jesus' Return 28, 168, 177
Jesus' Supremacy 105
Jesus' Understanding 182
Joy 197
Judgement 102
Judgment 186
Jurisdiction 110

King 96
Knowing God 26, 144

Law 174
Life 16, 53, 54
Life Mission 5
Life Needs 22
Life's Storms 47
Light 97

Like Christ 29
Lion's Share 105
Listening 13, 147
Living for Jesus 170
Living Water 61
Local Church 225
Longings 216
Look for Jesus 87
Lord's Supper 215
Love 86
Love of Jesus 88

Maintenance 83
Make Disciples 178
Marriage 81, 82, 83, 84, 86, 173
Meditation 189
Memory 43
Mercy 191
Messiah 159
Miracles 48
Money 232

Narrow Way 236
Needs 8, 132
New Creation 223
New Heart 108
New Life 6
New Work 1

Obedience 143
Obeying God 217
Obeying Jesus 145
Omniscience 196

Pain 182
Paradise 58
Partiality 239
Past 111, 223
Patience 121
Peace 246, 248
Peace of God 183
Perfection of Christ 55
Perfection of Jesus 68

Persistence 234
Perspective 40, 254
Pet Rocks 152
Plans 99
Plastic Jesus 261
Pleasing God 229
Poor in Spirit 34
Possessions 49
Postponement 42
Praise 89
Prayer 24, 67, 106, 142,
                    185, 226, 228, 234
Prayer Answered 185
Prejudice 239
Preparation 122
Priorities 25, 92
Procrastination 12
Purpose 120, 144, 180

Radiance 75
Reading the Bible 76, 188
Real Jesus 261
Redeemer 159
Redemption 111, 244
Relationships 60, 230
Remembrance 215
Repentance 201, 205
Reputation 208
Resolutions 157
Resources 156, 200
Responding to Jesus 251
Resurrection 63
Rest 9
Restoration 237, 244
Returns 201
Roadblocks 162
Rules 36

Sacrifice 56
Salvation 11, 51, 167, 171,
                    224, 240, 241, 251
Satan 135, 198, 218
Satisfaction 46, 152, 216

Saving Faith	240
Savior	159
Scripture	247
Scriptures	170
Seeking	235
Seeking God	104
Self-examination	190
Senses	109
Separation	163
Service	10
Serving	203
Serving Jesus	211
Set Free	71
Sex	236
Sexual Immorality	90
Sharing the Gospel	178
Sheep	233
Shepherding	233
Sight	43
Significance	204
Silent Night	248
Sin	179, 205
Sowing	50
Spider Man	170
Spiritual Gifts	203
Spiritual Health	214
Spiritual Leadership	164
Spiritual Warfare	98, 134
Stains	100
Storms	47
Strength	18, 175
Submission	85, 123
Success	151
Superheroes	200
Surprise	64
Surrender	16, 224

Temptation	17, 33, 35, 90, 139, 140, 150, 187, 218, 257
Thanking God	210
Time	39, 69
Tithing	129
Togetherness	10
Traditions	202
Trials	27, 138, 139
Tribulations	165
Trivial Pursuit	161
Trust	49, 95, 129
Trusting God	104, 213, 220
Trusting Jesus	166, 197
Truth	146
Victory	54
Vigilance of God	117
Vision	154
Victory	138
Walls	66
Wardrobe	128
Weakness	112, 182
Wealth	232
Wife	85
Wisdom	45, 250
Witness	230
Wives	173
Work	79
Works	27
World Perishing	53
Worry	3, 95
Worship	89
Worthiness	115
Zacharias, Ravi	193

OTHER BOOKS FROM STEPHEN NELSON RUMMAGE